AGAINST THE GRAIN

How I went From Factory Floor To My Own
Multi-million Pound Company (And How You Can Too)

Graham Harris

with

Mark Eglinton

AGAINST THE GRAIN

©Graham Harris 2018

Published in the UK in 2018 by Rudling House. A CIP catalogue record for this book is available from the British Library.

ISBN 978-1-910957-14-1

Cover design and typeset by Karen Ronan (coversbykaren.com)

www.rudlinghouse.com

RH

CONTENTS

Introduction

WHEN I was a twelve-year old school boy, there was a single moment that I feel sums up the message I am trying to convey in this book. It was my turn to read aloud in class one day – a few paragraphs of a book our teacher had chosen for us to study. All I remember was the fear of whether I would confidently speak the words clearly, or make a complete hash of them – as well as an awareness of some restless shuffles from disenchanted class mates and accompanying yawning sounds.

Then something out of the ordinary happened...

I found myself ignoring the words in front of me and instead I began ad-libbing the events to suit myself. I changed the characters, introduced more exciting ones – and I even described their colourful clothes before sending them off on a different, more fun adventure. As I continued I noticed the sound of almost every child in the room shuffling through the pages, desperately trying to find a place that didn't exist. The yawning stopped. I had their attention. As nervous and frightened as I was about venturing into unchartered territory; my teacher put me at ease as I glanced at her. She was smiling, and let me carry on for a few more minutes. I'd successfully changed a story written by someone else.

So, if you are in a situation, for one reason or another, where you feel you are living out a story written by someone else maybe a friend, colleague or manager who has scripted, with limitations, how they might see you in the next twenty years – my book will show you how wrong they could be. But it's down to how you react.

If you find yourself staring out of your kitchen, office or factory window dreaming of a better life but not knowing where to start in order to change its course, this book is perfect for you. Whether you are a full time mother/father at home, shop worker, builder, office or factory worker, aspiring entrepreneur or inventor, it doesn't matter. There's something here for you.

Whether you see yourself as an everyday person with little to offer the world, or feel cheated because your qualifications don't yet carry the weight you thought they would, my story will demonstrate how to re-think it all and build up your self-confidence in order to perhaps go against the grain by moving in a direction nobody could have ever predicted

I wanted to write about my story, mainly because it hasn't turned out quite the way I might have imagined as a twelve year old – or how some of my friends or colleagues might have scripted it. I took control of my life script, but only when I knew beyond doubt that I could make use of my creativity and forge my own path – and I feel you can learn to do the same when you've read about the various key turning points I faced.

Unlike some other inspirational business/entrepreneurial books about creativity and invention you may have read, I open up my mind and take you on the journey with me. And it's a really exciting journey. I want you to smile at my mistakes and calamities, be a little sad in the right places and cheer towards the end, not just for me, but for the hope and inspiration you might learn from my experience – all in the hope that you might start creating your own version of *your* story – a hugely successful one at that.

Believe me, if I can, you can too…

Prologue

WHILE OUT walking my dog on September 30th 2014, I received a message on my iPhone from my U.S. based lawyer. The preview gave nothing away, but the body of the email read like this: "I regret to say Judge Kendall granted Rosback's motion and denied ours: she found that Rosback does not infringe your '519 Patent."

Beyond that it guided me to a memorandum – a series of notes – that explained why the judge had ruled in favour of the defendant in a lawsuit we raised against a U.S. company called Rosback, whom we had deemed to be infringing my very first, ground breaking product. I could hardly bear to read these words. But I'd seen enough to know what it all meant.

At this point it's important to stress that I wasn't part of some large corporation that would particularly relish getting sucked into a drawn-out and costly legal battle. While there was some degree of provision in place for such an eventuality, my cash reserves still weren't exactly bottomless. I was Graham Harris – with no previous formal business experience prior to borrowing £2000 from my sister, to escape my position as an employee on someone else's factory floor, to get my fledgling company off the ground.

Escaping an unsatisfying working life comes with its stresses though – the main one being that I'd come to feel like my inventing career was some kind of stressful multi-chamber video game, with me, the main character, forging forward, always trying to stay a chamber or two ahead of my pursuers – desperate to stay in front and to keep this incredible dream alive. At times it was exhausting, and I literally did dream about being chased. And then now, having seemingly been reeled in by a pursuer, suddenly I felt wide open to threats that could significantly impact all that I'd worked so hard to create.

Receiving the email felt like someone had just pulled the plug on the whole game. In an instant, any degree of privilege I might have felt to be walking my dog in the Leicestershire countryside with friendly, smiling people all around me – happy children playing football – all gave way to a feeling of low dread. A black cloud descended. I was distraught. Suddenly, all my worst fears had reappeared.

The irony was, up until the precise moment that the message preview appeared on my phone screen, I was certain we'd win this case. And in the event that we didn't, we'd made appropriate financial provision for a bad outcome. Even after cat and mouse conversations with my attorney to establish exactly what chances *he* thought we had, even he had conceded, although never in writing, and always in suitably murky language, that the likelihood of a positive outcome was 'pretty high.' But in a court of law – particularly when you're British and in an American company's home court as it were – there are never any guarantees. In the days and weeks leading up to the outcome, I'd be lying if I said that thought hadn't occasionally crossed my mind.

The concept of stonewalling competition was hardly a new one. In the preceding years since my Eureka moment in 1999, it felt like I'd been fending off copycats left and right. Again, that tension is part of what motivates me. These threats came in various forms: a father and son at a German manufacturer called Heidelberg, who left the company to create their version of my Tri-Creaser. They sold a hundred units before a lawyer's letter triggered a hands-in-the-air 'it's a fair cop' apology from the father.

Then there was this cheeky gentleman who boasted that he had come up with a superior version of something I'd sweated blood to create. That's what people often claim: My product is cheaper, easier to use and gives better quality. That's never been the case and this person was stopped in his tracks. A few others mounted similar challenges.

You'd be entitled to ask why I bothered with all these imposters. Why not just focus on what's on my own plate?

Well, the primary concern is that someone might improve something they already had by extracting something from one of my patents – something that may have started out quite crude and basic, but could evolve into a significant threat. My instinct was always to stop that process before it went anywhere in terms of damaging my business. Paranoia about what others might be doing is an unsavoury part of what spurs me on to stay ahead. It drives me to levels I might not otherwise reach. Also, by taking all-comers on, I'd be sending a clear message to copiers that I wouldn't just stand aside and let them threaten my, my family's, my staff's and my distributor's livelihoods.

As a result, I'd become accustomed to the idea of *winning*. And despite the fact that this particular case only impacted my very first patent, which only had three or four years left to run, I hated the idea of losing now. The potential threat to our business and profits was just too significant to dismiss. Thinking about things logically, on reflection, this loss could have been worse. If there was ever a case to lose, this was probably it. But I still couldn't shake the sheer frustration of something not going my way – not to mention the realities associated with a quarter of a million pounds in legal fees.

The following morning, when the time came to tell my staff about the ruling, I found myself fighting back tears. On one hand I felt that somehow I had failed them. On another I was upset that I was showing vulnerability – something I wasn't in the habit of doing despite the fact that I always wore my heart on my sleeve when it came to passing on positive news to the staff. My feeling is that sharing good news lifts morale and makes a work force feel part of something bigger. To do that always felt good and came easily to me. But I had no idea how to articulate such negative news. I was wide open and raw with hurt.

Worse still was the fact that my lawyer said that the judge's memorandum was full of mistakes. And when I was calm enough to read the details of them myself I wholeheartedly agreed with him. But that didn't matter. The case was lost, and as if things couldn't get blacker, the possibility was raised that I could end up having to pay some or all of the defendant's legal and court fees in addition to my own. Knowing that my total costs could exceed £500,000 – and might even come closer to £1,000,000 – was enough to drain the colour from my face. There were potentially difficult times ahead.

But somehow in the days immediately following the ruling, I found a way to pull back from the edge of the abyss. In the back of my mind were stories and instances where other inventors' lives had been torn apart by a lawsuit going the wrong way. One guy I met in the U.S. had fought an Intellectual Property case and lost. His sons told me it destroyed him. He had heart attacks and other health issues. I didn't want to go down that path and as my wife, Sue, who is also our financial director, correctly pointed out that 'nobody died.' As hard as it can be sometimes, when the negative thoughts are at the forefront, those people that are successful in business over a long period will always put things in perspective.

I made a concerted decision to park the negativity and get on with business. We'd lost the case and I took ownership of that. No excuses and certainly no regrets at the idea of taking the case on to defend what was mine. But at the same time, the emotions I felt when threatened only spurred me on to work harder, *fight* harder, to develop the business and stick to my mantra of having a dream and making it come true. I needed to reinstate my confidence in the technology I had created. I had to keep moving through the chambers.

Without realising it, I was learning more about myself. I may appear shy and quiet because I'm not the type to blow my own trumpet, but my steel and resolve even surprises me at times. I seem to find a way to navigate problems, not dwell on the negatives for too long and then keep moving forward. I realised that I had a wonderful life with so much opportunity far beyond anything I'd ever imagined – and I wasn't about to let a litigation case pull me down into the mire. The hard truth is, business is business and an inventor has to know his stuff. Litigation goes with the territory – particularly if you've unearthed a money-making idea – and its effects can lead to heartbreak if you let it. But inventing is only a small part of my business; there's so much more to do every day and my focus was that.

Even the tricky part of dealing with the defendant's

gloating press release, was something I viewed as an opportunity for a positive spin. After all, I had never hesitated to bring out a press release to let the world know of *my* past victories and to expose those who had crossed my company. But now I was on the receiving end, and boy did they wallow in their moment of glory: *Rosback defeats Technifold in a landmark patent case...*

All I could do was take it on the chin...

Three magazine editors contacted me for comment. And after consultation with my lawyer I delivered what I thought were some pretty good responses. I saw this as my time to deflect the negatives with a positive from our side. I mentioned that – although this case involved our very first patent, which accounted for less than 1% of our annual profits – we believe in fighting for our IP no matter what. In the face of defeat I wasn't flinching. I was standing strong.

And then I finished by announcing our newly patented technology that was far superior to its predecessor. I was asked to supply some product images with a summary of features and we got some free publicity – it wasn't all bad news. The chase was on again.

Chapter 1

Something More

SOME PEOPLE are naturally blessed with great talent. And those individuals usually follow the path laid out for them and often do extremely well in life – sometimes without appearing to ever have to work especially hard at it. I am *not* one of those people – and if you're not one of them either, keep reading. This book is for you.

If anything I am the diametric opposite of these types. I can lay claim to no dazzling innate talent. Because I'm naturally shy and the epitome of ordinary, I tend to blend into the background and to dodge the path most taken. Yet, despite this seemingly retiring nature, I still always dreamed of doing something extraordinary with my life. The hardest part was answering the biggest question of all: *how?*

I've thought about this continually and, over time, I've come to realise that people like 'us' must look far beyond the status quo to find our own niche. We must push against convention and what the majority deem to be normal. Be in no doubt: we have our place in this world – for sure we do. But we must work diligently and cleverly to create our opportunities. My life has been a constant fight against adversity, barriers and, at times, myself. Let me rewind and tell you where it began...

When I snatched a skipping rope from Johnny Penner as an eight-year old child back in 1971, my innocent mind could never have contemplated what would happen next. Johnny told his cousins, Danny and Jez Kowaski, about the incident and my life changed in an instant. Danny was the quiet bully – he used his clever words and aggressive posture to lay down constant threats without actually striking out. Jez just went for it; he hit kids for the sheer fun of it. Now they had a joint project to work on, and that project was me: the tall, shy, skinny kid who had upset their cousin.

Danny and Jez had a circle of friends, and they all helped form an impressive alliance – which basically meant that I never found a moment's peace. It started with a baptism of fire as Jez floored me from behind during playtime one day. And before any teachers were to be seen, lasting damage was done – damage that would follow me through life like a spectre. Jez smashed my head like someone smashing a coconut. But it wasn't milk that seeped out. It was my self-esteem and confidence that drained away.

Going home after school was always complicated. Danny's mates often lay in wait, behind trees, cars or down alleys – they would leap out without warning and take a cheap shot. Break time and play time turned into a hunting game, with me being 'the hunted'. Worse still, the hunters' membership was growing and hiding places for me were becoming few and far between. But as scared as I was, I wouldn't give in. As time passed I found ways of deflecting attacks and in doing so I realised that I was thwarting their attempts to become that day's hero. I even found ways to lash back, subtly at first, but with increasing effect as time went on.

Then something amazing happened...

My parents purchased one of the very first, colour television sets in the neighbourhood. Immediately, bully-boy Danny called a ceasefire whilst he and Jez investigated how they might capitalise. Within a day or two Danny and Jez became regular visitors to the

Harris household and, all of a sudden, I had two "false friends" (albeit that I've given them fabricated names here). Unwittingly, my parents had happened upon a solution, although they never knew they needed to.

Although there was a deep-rooted sadness to this aspect of my childhood, I always wanted to keep it hidden and in its place. But unbeknown to me, with retrospect, these stressful events signalled the beginning of my developing, subconsciously, an unusually tough interior that was in stark contrast to my shy demeanour. Looking back on all this now, I've even managed to put a positive spin on it all, to the extent that I now like to think of my upbringing as being happy – with loving parents and many friends. Nevertheless, the origins of the tough interior are significant.

The amusing thing is, at first glance, nothing about me, or my upbringing, could be viewed as a precursor to the outstanding achievement I always envisioned for myself. My twin brother, Peter, and I were the youngest of four children born to Michael and Betty Harris. We lived in a tiny house in a working-class neighbourhood of Leicester, England, 90 miles from London. When I was eleven, we moved to a larger semi-detached house in a middle-class neighbourhood, which, in retrospect, we thought was quite fancy. On one hand I was glad that my parents finally had the lovely home they deserved, but even at that young age, I recognised the considerable sacrifices they'd made to get there.

I wouldn't want to say that my parents' admirable work ethic ever detracted from our upbringing, but my siblings and I often had to fend for ourselves because our parents worked many hours, including some evenings, and often had to take extra jobs to provide for our family. For many years, our father worked on the assembly line at the local hosiery factory – a job he did well but with little enthusiasm and for a modest wage. Later he landed a job selling insurance, which brought him both a better pay cheque and greater satisfaction.

During our early childhoods, our mother worked as many hours as she could – forgoing her secretarial training to clean other people's houses so that she would be available to take care of us. Sometimes our dad worked from home so that she could work more than just part-time hours. Consequently, Mum was often so tired in the evenings from juggling her job with raising four children and running a household that she'd fall asleep exhausted on the couch.

Nevertheless, neither of my parents ever complained about how hard they worked or about their station in life. Instead, their entire focus was on providing a good life for their family, not on keeping up with the Joneses. And they did what they could with humility, integrity, and grace. With retrospect, those virtues are the most valuable gifts they could have ever given me – along with their permission and constant encouragement to be myself. And that was no small gift; I was a bird of a different feather on most levels.

Visually, I was skinny and tall for my age, half a head above my twin brother. My gangly stature set me apart from my peers and only added to my awkwardness and shyness. Only in my late teens – when I began to fill out a bit and when some of my peers were tall enough that I no longer towered over them – did I feel less self-conscious about my height.

Being over six feet tall also gave me some advantage on the rugby field however. I wasn't as good at rugby as I would have liked, though – mainly because the game has too many rules and I've always had inbuilt urge to succeed by always going against the accepted way of doing things. On the rugby pitch, that sometimes meant using my speed to run the ball into touch if I couldn't score – in order to at least gain 50 yards instead of settling for the 10 yards my teammate would've got through slicing his kick. Such single-minded purpose does not always fare well in a sport in which a team must perform such choreographed moves and adhere to steadfast rules. As I took off on another one of my mazy runs – my teammates would often be left scratching their heads.

On all fronts, from an early age, I resisted convention and conformity and prized individuality and creativity instead. As a child, I had a heart for trying to be creative but I never quite pulled it off. My first "invention," if you could call it that, at the age of six, was a cardboard dispenser that dropped a sweet into a tray when a penny was inserted. I had little time to enjoy my creative triumph, however, as my brother ripped apart my sweet machine and took all the sweets without paying.

Another of my early creations stands out in my memory because of both the ingenuity that went into it, and how my young pride was hurt because of it. I was eight years old, and my school was holding a fete that included a fancy dress competition. I wanted to enter, but my mum didn't have time to put together an outfit for me. So I decided to make my own and looked through a book for ideas. When I spotted a photograph of a Beefeater (a Yeoman guard of the Royal Palace and the Tower of London), dressed to the nines in his colourful and regal uniform, my imagination soared. I decorated a cake tin and added a cardboard rim to make the hat. Then I draped a red blanket around me and completed my outfit with a pair of knee-high red socks and some wellington boots.

At school, a teacher instructed all of the children who were participating in the fancy dress competition to form a line because those students didn't have to pay the fee for the event. I happily joined the line of costumed children. The first blow came when I was told to go to the queue where children and adults were waiting to pay. Thankfully, a friend's mum kindly gave me the entrance fee. Once inside, I joined the circle of students dressed to impress and parading around. I'd only taken a few steps when I felt the teacher's hand on my shoulder from behind, pulling me out of the parade. Crushed and confused as to why my outfit hadn't made the grade, I sadly made my way home.

That disheartening experience did not dampen my spirits for long though.

Nor did it stifle my imagination or my exuberance for marching to the beat of my own drum. An autobiography I produced as a class assignment sticks in my mind. Even though I had only eleven years of life to write about, it still seemed like an enormous task. But I loved doing it and took the liberty of including lots of photographs. I got top marks for that project and was very proud of it. The next year, however – when I looked at the masterpiece through my twelve-year old eyes – it didn't live up to my newfound standards, and so I ripped it up. That trait has stayed with me to this day; I am rarely completely satisfied with the products I develop and am on a constant quest to improve them.

I'd like to say I put as much heart and hard work into all my schoolwork as I did that autobiography assignment, but that just wasn't the case. I was often pulled up for not applying myself and for not taking school seriously enough. Even in my strong subjects, English and Art, I put in minimal effort and was easily disenchanted. It was never enough for me to do well at something; I wanted to be the best. On one occasion, after seeing a friend's drawing in class and thinking how amazing it was and how gifted he was, my own enthusiasm for drawing waned. As a result, my performance in school never went much beyond average.

It wasn't that I was a bad student though. I was respectful of my teachers and classmates, and I got good enough grades to pass. I just didn't study or revise for exams, and I fooled around and bent the rules. Furthermore, even to my developing mind, the state school system fostered conformity and discouraged creativity. Basically I had no interest in school and felt it had little to offer me in return – and my parents didn't push my siblings or I to excel academically anyway. So by the time I'd finished my compulsory education at the age of sixteen, I just wanted to get a job. And so I did – with my parents' blessing and, to my horror, my mum's help.

"Here's to the crazy ones. The misfits. The rebels. The troublemakers. The round pegs in the square holes. The ones who see things differently. They're not fond of rules. And they have no respect for the status quo. And while some may see them as the crazy ones, we see genius. Because the people who are crazy enough to think they can change the world are the ones who usually do." — Steve Jobs

Paying My Dues, Learning the Ropes

Rather embarrassingly for me, my mother got me my first job interview. My mum – shy and soft-spoken as she was meant to be – simply rang up the owner of a local print finishing company, Senator Print Finishers, and asked whether he might be interested in hiring her son, who had just finished his secondary school education and had absolutely no training or work experience in print finishing.

She'd been looking through job vacancies without me even knowing. I don't know what she said that persuaded him to give me the interview, and I have no idea what transpired during the interview to convince him to give me a job. I went to that interview not having a clue what a print finisher even did, but regardless, I turned up for my first day of work eager to learn all about it.

I spent the first week picking up the trimmed paper that spewed out of the machines used to trim and bind the pages of books, filling bin after bin with the endless flow of waste. Other similarly laborious tasks were added to my responsibilities, and although I did my job well and without complaint, my innate desire to elevate myself soon kicked in.

That's when I began to take notice of the way the skilled operators set up their machines to produce a complementary finish to beautifully printed pieces. The complicated and exacting process of collating, folding, stitching, and trimming hundreds of thousands of printed sheets always held the threat of something going wrong, with the result that the whole printed piece sometimes had to be entirely reprinted – at a cost of thousands of pounds. The culprit might be something as simple as a scuff mark showing up on the page of the brochure because someone had failed to clean an ink spot on a fold roller, or it could have been that the spine of the book cover showed signs of cracking because the crease we'd applied wasn't deep enough.

My respect for those craftsmen only grew as I watched them masterfully perform the intricate processes and surmount the complex challenges of print finishing. I paid particular attention to the operators of the paper-folding machines, which required the highest level of skill to master. Many times I asked the best operators questions about the methods they utilized to solve some of the most challenging print-finishing tasks in Europe – finishing jobs that many other U.K. companies were unable to perform with any degree of success. Unfortunately, the experienced technicians and operators blatantly refused to share their knowledge with younger workers like me. It even seemed as if those guys we looked up to somehow saw us as a threat and so denied us trainees any opportunity to learn from their experience.

I had no choice but to teach myself...

As an assistant with the job of packing finished products, I would stand as close as possible to the top operators, just to study their technical abilities and problem-solving techniques. Beyond that I also volunteered to work overtime on weekends, venturing that the longer hours would increase my chances of filling-in for older workers who needed to be at home with their families.

In this way, I slowly progressed – first learning how to handle paper and load the feeding sections of folding machines. There was a fine art to this important process, and on weekends, when some of the operators didn't work, I took that opportunity to hone my skills.

Our bosses would tell us youngsters that apprenticeships were a waste of time, that there was nothing like being "thrown into the deep end" and learning your craft through hands-on experience and by conquering tough production issues on the fly. They often pointed to time-served certified apprentices who'd joined the company but "couldn't hack it" and left as "failures." As if to back that theory up they would then point out guys two years older than me who had blossomed into skilled operators through their "system" of "learning by doing."

As I began to operate machines and develop my craft, I suppose I understood what they meant. But I still always felt lacking and vulnerable. I used to think that maybe an apprenticeship certificate would at least tell the world I had accomplished something of worth and give me more confidence. After all, I had secured this job with no qualifications (and I wondered, should I ever want or need to move on to another company, whether my not having "official" qualifications would prove to be my Achilles heel).

I also began to wonder if I had enough talent to ever make it into the higher echelon of operators in the company. The supervisors did nothing to bolster my confidence. In that first job, I had two bosses. One was straight-talking and hard-driving. He was a tough taskmaster and was quick to anger and sometimes swore at us. Regardless, we knew what he wanted and we respected him. Although he pushed us, he still had it in him to buy us fish and chips and share a whiskey with him at the end of a long, hard day. The other boss loved criticizing us, usually behind our backs. He lorded over us underlings, never missing an opportunity to put us in our place or humiliate us. It was bad cop, bad cop.

In retrospect, we were exploited in the sense that we worked long hours for the lowest wages in the company and with no training or support from management. At the time, I was grateful to have a job at all – in a respectable trade that paid modestly. So, despite the downsides, I hung in there and tried to make the most of the situation. There seemed to be no alternative. And had I just walked out – like some of my fellow trainees who couldn't handle the gruelling hours and the mistreatment of our bosses – I probably wouldn't be where I am today. The unavoidable fact was that Senator Print Finishers was the best print-finishing company in Europe, and working on some of the most difficult print-finishing projects in the U.K. helped me to develop the skills and confidence I'd need to chart my own course, when the time was right.

Meanwhile, I did enjoy some aspects of the job, and I was earning more than most of my friends. Of course, I was also working 60 to 80 hours a week in a job that was both physically and mentally taxing. While my friends had an abundance of time and energy to hit the nightclubs on weekends but no cash to do it, I was in the opposite situation. I had plenty of cash in hand but no energy or time to go out on the town to spend any of it. I also had the ever-imminent 6:00 am start on Sunday morning...

A little depressingly perhaps, even at that tender age, I suspected that my friends would likely catch up with me in a few years and go on to out-earn me in less strenuous and more prestigious positions – unless, of course, I found a way to improve my prospects. However, before I could address that, something happened that would force my hand.

Because my opportunities for socialising were constrained somewhat by my working hours, with retrospect, when I did get the chance to go out with my mates I probably tried too hard to make up for lost time. Consequently, I certainly drank more than I should have on a few occasions. On one such night, I remember hearing whispers being exchanged between a consultant and a nurse in what I had learnt a few hours later was a hospital recovery room, to where I'd just been brought having undergone emergency surgery.

One was telling the other that he was surprised I was alive, and casually stated that if I wasn't so drunk I would probably be in the morgue. Apparently my more relaxed body posture, due to the heavy alcoholic intake, had actually saved my life. My body had taken the full force of the car as it hit me full on. My head took a hit too as I was tossed like a rag doll to the ground, but my tongue cushioned the full force of the impact while my teeth badly lacerated my tongue. Had I seen the car coming and braced myself, my life would have been snuffed out at the age of nineteen. I'm ashamed to admit that I'd been attempting to cross a busy road by dodging traffic.

This needless accident made me realise several things: who my real friends were – who I loved and who loved me back. I couldn't talk to any of them because my tongue had been stitched and stapled to my upper lip. But I could see the various emotions in their eyes – not all of them what I expected. My parents particularly went through hell and my emotions went haywire when – as battered, painful reality returned with my sobriety – I realised what I'd put them through and felt the depth of our mutual love.

My feelings about many of my friends and the

24

pointless lifestyle I could easily envisage living with them if I didn't recognise a fork in the road, changed in an instant. I could have added to their bank of funny stories by turning up at the pub a few weekends later like a circus act with a black, disfigured tongue to show for a road traffic accident that almost killed me. But, as the part of my tongue that was stitched back on died, my desire for the typical 'beers with the lads' life expired with it. As tough a decision as it was, I chose not to go to the pub. Instead, I went against the grain. I gave up smoking, discarded some of the less necessary friends and dedicated more time to getting myself fit playing rugby.

In retrospect I've come to realise that many life lessons are rolled up in this near death experience. In making the decision to diverge from this familiar path, I was about to invent my own personal version of my own life. It was one that I alone would control and direct, no matter how difficult it was or how long it might take. The speech therapist told me I'd need six months of therapy to learn how to speak again. I went to one session and then dedicated myself, in my own time, to getting rid of the lisp I'd been left with. I recognised the early signs of getting off track in an attempt to fit in with the crowd. As a result I realised that I needed to depend less on others and more on myself. I needed to forge my own path.

A Distant Dream

By my early twenties, I could operate the folding and finishing machines at a higher-than-average level, thanks to the complexity of work we took on and to the tips and tricks I'd picked up along the way. That

25

is also when my obsession with developing alternative methods of solving print-finishing problems kicked in.

This obsession was born out of three realities: my inbuilt fear of being average, my desire to make my own job easier, and my recognition of how far up the company pecking order I could realistically expect to climb based on my skills alone.

The problem was, in order to be considered the cream of the crop and, consequently, to attract better wages, you needed to be among the top four operators out of a crew of sixteen. I knew at least two people who were that good, and in pitting my skills against the best craftsmen in our company, I figured I ranked about fifth, on a good day. On that basis I realized that there was no way I could break into the top group based on talent alone, so I decided to focus on devising ways to do things more efficiently.

Via my silent observations, I'd noticed that the best operators followed the established set-up procedure to which most print finishers adhere. Granted, those guys probably could have performed that set-up procedure with their eyes shut, and they never varied from those "tried and tested" methods. That was one of their greatest strengths but also a weakness. The trouble with rigidly following procedures in general is that when they fail you, as one day they will, there isn't always a Plan B in place. Furthermore, when the established procedures didn't produce acceptable results for these seasoned operators, those problematic jobs either significantly slowed down output or didn't get done at all – and both had a negative impact on company profits, as the angrier of our two bosses never failed to let us know. So, with all these factors in my mind, I was always trying to figure out alternative ways to achieve good or better results.

For example, one day our best operator was struggling to fold a particular leaflet. We had 5 million to produce. To meet our delivery deadline, the output rate should have been averaging 12,000 finished leaflets per hour, but he was averaging only 2,000. The consensus was that if that was the best this highly skilled operator could do – then it was unthinkable that anyone else could better his rate. I had a different take on the situation.

Here, I thought, *is my chance to steal some limelight.*

The reason that the top operator was struggling was because all of the sheets were ridden with static charges (a by-product of web press speeds), which would randomly cause a sheet to miss the fold plate and, in turn, jam the machine. He had applied all the standard tricks for combating static problems, such as dampening the roller and using an anti-static bar to defuse the charges, but with only partial success.

I noticed the guillotine operator was cutting the sheets into single copies so I asked my manager if I could place an untrimmed ream of sheets on my machine to fold and trim in one pass. My theory was that by doing so I might reduce the static charges, or at least thinly spread them so that the sheets wouldn't miss the fold plate. The set-up was complicated and involved adding cutting tools, separately scoring every three copies, and sending them to a second unit to be folded in the opposite direction.

By the time I'd finished the set-up, four hours later, my manager was on the brink of pulling the plug altogether. Fortunately, he didn't. And soon my machine began processing flawless sheets at an average rate of

18,000 per hour and the top two operators were asked to reset their machines to the format I had created. Together, the three of us were able to output 54,000 perfectly folded leaflets per hour, as opposed to 6,000 poorly finished versions using the standard set-up.

Another couple of similarly successful set-ups got me moved into the elusive top four, which equated to more recognition and money.

That's when it occurred to me that my creative way of thinking might give me an edge in my profession. I am a realist. I recognize and work to my strengths. Similarly, I acknowledge and circumnavigate my weaknesses. For example, at one point in my twenties, I dreamed about becoming a first-class rugby player. In reality, I was much better with the ball than without it, good at scoring points but not so great at tackling. Besides, at that time rugby wasn't a professional sport; players only profited through sponsorship, and I needed a more reliable source of income. So really it was just wishful thinking.

Meanwhile, my childhood fantasy of doing something extraordinary was getting some traction in my job. At work, unlike in school and in rugby, my penchant for finding better ways of doing things had the potential to move me tangibly ahead. Plus, I relished the challenge of developing innovative solutions to sticky problems.

To the outside world, I guess I didn't have the kind of job that seemed exciting or that my friends could identify with – but I really loved going to work and teaching myself some obscure but effective set-up procedures. Time used to fly by as I brainstormed and tested out my methods to increase speed of output and to improve finished quality. Sometimes my methods failed, but to me those misses just added to my growing databank of what worked and didn't work.

When the better of my two bosses left to head up another print-finishing company, I followed him to be his foreman. A few years later, when that company was on the brink of bankruptcy due to our main customer going into liquidation, I returned to Senator Print Finishers as the manager of their subsidiary in a different town. Despite my new title and responsibilities, I still felt like the low man on the totem pole – even after I had landed a major contract for the company.

The five-year contract was with *Reader's Digest*, and every major printing company and print-finishing company in Europe had bid on the job, but none had produced an acceptable finished sample. The brochure was printed on lightweight paper that was riddled with static. The finishing process included trimming off 8 millimetre edges, which isn't easy to do on good quality paper let alone poor quality, and then folding the printed piece at different angles. Our top operators at our main factory had given up, and their manager drove over to show me the sample and to see whether I had any ideas for solving the problem.

I revelled at the challenge. I was their last hope. I sensed the bosses were expecting to make that call to the customer to say we'd failed. But I wasn't to be beaten. I looked at every aspect of the process and from all angles and tried many different things, putting in hours and hours of my own time. When I finally managed to produce several good copies, it was the best feeling in the world. And we got the contract as a result. It was one of the most profitable jobs we took on – to the extent that we had one machine devoted to it twenty-four hours a day, sometimes seven days a week, for five years.

But if it was recognition or adulation I was looking for, they didn't come.

As a result of my efforts the company won a national award for producing the most sophisticated and complex print-finishing product that year. My bosses went to the trade show to collect the award and take the glory. It all happened without me even knowing, and I didn't get as much as a thank you or any type of acknowledgement from my bosses.

I won't deny that the lack of acknowledgement stung a little. No one likes to feel taken for granted. But I shrugged off my disappointment because I realized the upside of the situation. I had taken on and conquered a task at which the top craftsman in all the leading print-finishing operations in Europe had failed. *I* was the one who had worked out how to solve a seemingly impossible problem. I was the only one who knew every permutation that I'd tried and with what results. Significantly too, the experience reinforced how grit, determination and out-of-the-box thinking can get you over the line. I was beginning to feel that my own self-taught apprenticeship and my unconventional approach to my trade might get me somewhere, some day.

I'd also learned another big lesson that would help me in later life: how not to be a boss and how not to run a company. Praise from management was few and far between at the best of times, and one of our bosses deliberately set out to make operators look foolish. One of his tactics was to distract an operator and speed up the machine while he was looking away; this happened to me twice. Some of my co-workers felt demoralized, and you could see they were giving only enough to get them through.

When I was managing the subsidiary, the same

boss who routinely humiliated his subordinates tried to impress me by humiliating the temping staff manager. After one temp worker turned up an hour late for the shift I was running, this boss called the temp agency and exaggerated the situation. He ranted and bullied until the temp manager agreed to send over two temps for free the next day. I felt embarrassed for that poor temp worker and sick to the pit of my stomach at my boss's attitude and behaviour. I vowed that if I ever had my own business, I would never stoop so low as that.

Of course, at the time, owning my own business was nothing more than a fleeting fantasy. When you are a young person without formal qualifications or certificates to your name, working in a factory or some other mundane job, it's easy to be insular, thinking that your immediate world is your only world. It's easy to become trapped by what you deem to be your lot in life and it takes monumental effort and focus to plot your way out of those confines and to create a vision of something better, somewhere else. This effort is fuelled by a desire to do something special and anyone reading this book that has those same feelings, need only apply the same kind of resolve.

So I concentrated on honing my craft with a view to working my way up the ranks. But that only took me so far. Even though I'd made it to the number-four spot in the pecking order, no one I worked with would have put me among the most talented or skilled print finishers. In my late twenties, I began to realize that as long as I worked for someone else, my opportunities would be limited. For the first time, I could envision getting out of the factory and striking out on my own. Sensing my time was yet to come, I continued to accumulate ideas that I was sure would one day help make that dream a reality. I was like a magpie gathering fodder for the future.

> *"Opportunity is missed by most people because it is dressed in overalls and looks like hard work."* — Thomas Edison

The Turning Point

When the subsidiary of Senator Print Finishers closed, I was offered the manager position at the main facility. By then, my desire to progress in the company had vanished along with my respect for my bosses. So I declined the offer and instead returned to the factory as a print finisher, planning to stick it out only until I could find a way to break from the company where I would always be thought of as the young trainee, no matter how far up the ladder I climbed.

Starting a business of my own was increasingly on my mind. I was already working hard and long hours, often on weekends, and missing out on too many family activities. I wanted to earn the same or more money by working fewer hours, and I didn't want to be held back by someone else's business-as-usual attitude and preconceived notions of my abilities.

My first try at my own business sank before the wind even caught its sails, but I learned some important lessons while it lasted. The idea was to buy and sell print-finishing equipment. I figured I could dip my toe in to see if anything came of it while I continued to work at my day job. So I found a classified ad in a trade magazine for a reconditioned miniature, folding machine, a fairly rare piece of equipment used to fold pharmaceutical instructions and documentation, for only £1,500. I made an appointment with the seller, a printer in Brighton, and gave the machine the once-over. Then, I asked my parents if they could lend me the money until I'd sold the machine. They agreed, and I will never discount their trust and belief in me. I purchased the machine and stored it in my garage until I could find a buyer.

Then, I got the notion that I could maybe rig up the machine and do contract jobs on it myself on the side. I ran the idea past a trusted colleague. He reckoned I could pull it off, and he and another person offered to join me. Unfortunately (or, in retrospect, fortunately), one of those "trusted" friends told my boss about my scheme, and I was summoned to the office that was usually reserved for meetings with our top customers.

As I took that long walk, I felt the eyes of everyone piercing my back and my chest tightening with dread. I knew I was in deep trouble and that this was going to end badly, with me possibly being fired on the spot. My boss didn't reveal his source, and I came clean straight away, leaning more on my plan to resell the machine than on the part about starting up as his rival. His face was red with anger, but he kept it under control. I even detected some concern at how far I might have taken this idea. I apologized and promised to sell the machine, and no more was ever said. On the way back to my station, I wondered who might have tipped off my boss. But it didn't haunt me for long because I realized they'd really done me a favour.

Although I'd risked losing my job only to have my plan pulled out from under me, I consoled myself that at least I'd tried to change my life. When my plan came crashing down around my ears, those who had opted in to help me disappeared into the background, leaving me to carry the can. I held no bad feelings; upon reflection I realized that they were just protecting their own skin. But it also taught me that, no matter how excited you might be about your idea for a new business or product, discussing it with even your closest colleagues or friends is rarely in your best interests. *In my experience, it is far better to develop the concept in private and take it through the many phases of development before letting the world know about it.* From that point on, I was even more alienated from my bosses and management. I felt like a jailed prisoner who had bodged an attempted escape and was under 24–hour watch.

I had also set myself apart from some of my work friends, too. A few seemed almost eager for me to put my head in the noose and hang myself. I doubt many, if any, would have gambled on me ever being successful.

Trying to launch a business or a product inevitably involves some measure of risk.

And you have to be brave enough and tough enough to take it on the chin if it doesn't work out. You pick yourself up, dust yourself off, and start all over again.

And so I did.

I sold the miniature, folding machine for double what I'd paid for it. My wife, Sue, and I repaid my parents and took them out for a meal to thank them. We tried to share the profit with them, but they refused anything more than what they'd lent us. With the profit, Sue and I bought a lovely new log fireplace.

About a year later, I left Senator to take a job as the finishing manager at Streamline Press. Over the next few years, a couple of other of my business ideas came and went, never really getting off the ground. Looking back now, I realize how naïve and unprepared I was anyway. I had no real business plan and no money behind me. But I have no regrets because those "failed" attempts to start my own business taught me some valuable lessons and proved that I could make money and take risks. My dream was bruised but not broken.

Then, on a cold November morning in 1998, everything about the way I thought about life changed.

While I sat in my car waiting to start my shift, a dark mood crept over me. I tried to work out why I was feeling so low – while at the same time trying to motivate myself to make it through that day. As I sat, staring through the rain-soaked windscreen, I reflected on how much I had loved the practical and creative side of my work, brainstorming solutions to technical problems and getting my hands dirty to achieve a result that even the finishing-equipment manufacturers claimed was impossible. Now, instead, the bulk of my time was spent trying to solve people problems – organizing overtime, sorting out petty issues, addressing performance deficits, dealing with employees' personal problems – like an operator who came to work under the influence of alcohol. Although I am a compassionate and understanding person and was adept at all of the above, I realised that I missed the hands-on involvement with production more than anything.

Here I was, thirty-six years old and had worked my way up to middle management. I'd been hired to build a finishing department and to assemble a team of specialists to assist me in running it. That part of the job had been accomplished a year or so earlier, and I had been going through a period of reflection, wondering whether the grey-haired version of me would still be planning out work schedules some twenty years later.

That possibility really scared me.

It wasn't the idea of traditional hard work that bothered me. But I definitely felt like my whole attitude to the act of *being* an employee was in question as I sat there. Call me old-fashioned, but I have always believed in putting in a good day's work for one's employer. I used to be amazed at the lackadaisical attitudes of many colleagues throughout the years. Some would constantly come in late. Many would watch the clock until it struck the magic time signalling the end of their shift and then announce, "I'm out of this dump." And, for the first time in my life, I was experiencing similar feelings. I had to act. It felt like now or never.

Previously, I had persuaded my wife, Sue, to help me register a company name in case I came up with an idea to start a business. I began to pop in on local printing companies after my day job to advise them on technical issues relating to folding machines – mainly for my own experience and usually for free. After working on one such project, the owner felt he should pay me. We sent the invoice under our newly formed and named company, Tech-ni-Fold. That alone represented a big step towards freedom. As time passed, I began to sense that I might be onto something. But I felt that I still needed something more tangible to help me make the complete shift to being an independent entity – either by creating a cutting-edge training program based on my experience, or, better still, a breakthrough process or product that would save my future customers time and money.

As I walked from my car to the factory, I reminded myself of the positive aspects of my job. My present boss was different from my previous bosses; he treated me well and allowed me to run my department the way

I felt was right. I was paid pretty well and had good prospects going forward. I was married with two young children, and this job gave us security and a good life.

Then, with a jolt, I realized that, as good as all that sounded, it wasn't enough for me. The thought of staying in a "nice and safe" job for the rest of my working days left me with an empty feeling. Again, I was struck with the desire to put all I'd taught myself over the past 20 years to practice in my own business. But I didn't know how or where to start.

A few days later, as if I needed any more encouragement, one of our finishing assistants, "Fireman Mick," who worked part-time for us when he wasn't on duty at the fire station, told me about a fellow fireman who had developed a potentially life-saving device and was offered £500,000 outright for his patent. That story didn't end well because when his colleague pushed for a cool million, the manufacturer withdrew the offer and went on to develop a similar product.

Although Mick's colleague had missed out, I loved hearing about a regular guy who had invented a device with the potential to save lives *and* to improve his life. Hearing his story inspired me. It also changed the way I thought about how I might use my creativity and my passion for problem solving, which until then I'd thought might only ever benefit my bosses. Then and there, I set my sights on forging a new path to a better life – as an inventor...

Chapter 2

Ticket to Paradise

WHEN FIREMAN MICK told me about his colleague being offered more than a half-million pounds for his invention, it reminded me of how good it had felt when I'd bought the folding machine and sold it at a profit in my first, embryonic attempt at starting a business. Something about the simplistic nature of the transaction: selling something at a profit and reaping the benefit, must have appealed to the entrepreneurial side of me

Before hearing about Mick's inventor friend, I'd never even considered inventing a product other than when I was a child. But I can't deny that the conversation resonated with me and, in turn, reignited my passion to strike out on my own. As such, I began to fantasize about the prospect of inventing something that solved a major problem in the print-finishing industry and then selling my idea for millions. But then I'd come back down to earth and reason that, as a compromise, maybe if I could come up with an improvement to an existing piece of equipment that might enable me to start my own consultancy and training business. That seemed a more realistic starting point.

Nevertheless, it seemed strangely fitting that Mick had told me about his colleague's invention while we were seated on a couple of dusty pallets of paper during our thirty-minute lunch break – in the midst of a work environment that had many inherent and unresolved problems. My challenge was to find a problem that I could solve and that printing companies would be willing to pay serious money for.

And I dared to dream big...

"Anything that won't sell, I don't want to invent. Its sale is proof of utility, and utility is success."— Thomas Edison

Finding A Problem To Solve

Unlike most inventors who come up with a big idea and then try to find a market for it, I set out to identify that one big problem for which existing solutions were inadequate or absent. And since my area of expertise related to folding machines, that seemed a logical place to start.

In layman's terms, a folding machine automatically folds various sizes of sheets of paper upon which a book, flyer, menu, or other document has been printed. In addition, all leading brands of commercial folding machines are supplied with a series of accessory tools designed for the various functions of cutting, micro perforating, and scoring paper. These *rotary* (rotating) devices attach to the folding machine, and each performs a specific duty either before or after the sheet is folded. A *cutting* tool trims the sheet to the required size. A *micro-perforating* tool creates tiny holes where a coupon, order form, or similar portion of the sheet can be torn off. A *scoring* tool creates a slight indentation where the sheet will be folded.

I realized that any fundamental problems with the folding machines themselves either had been, were being, or would be addressed by the machine manufacturers – most of them huge corporations in Germany, the largest being Heidelberg. So instead I decided to focus on the accessory tools themselves. From reading trade magazines and from talking with the salespeople and technicians who sold and installed folding machines, I knew about all the latest and forthcoming products. And nothing was on the horizon designed to improve the functionality of these rather crude accessory tools that were so crucial to a print finisher's working day.

I recalled all of the difficulties that I, along with every print finisher I'd ever worked with, had encountered when using the accessory tools supplied with folding-machine packages. The biggest problem, by far, was associated with rotary scoring devices. These tools usually worked fine for their intended purpose: to score paper. But they rarely worked well for the heavier duty card stock typically used for book covers, menus, and greeting cards – in which case the fibres along the score almost always *cracked* (separated) when the paper was folded. This cracking issue was particularly troublesome and pronounced on heavy stocks that were printed in darker inks (coated with varnish or a similar substance to produce a sharper image).

From an aesthetic standpoint, cracking can ruin the look of the book, and in this case print customers really *do* judge a book by its cover. After all, a printing or print-finishing company might typically pay £50,000 to £90,000 for a folding machine, only to have the scoring tool either cut the sheet in half or apply a score that damaged the fibres and led to cracking along the fold.

Of course, as stated in every manufacturer's operating manual, a paper-folding machine is meant to fold paper and only paper, not card stock, and its accessory tools are meant to aid in that function and only that function. But that didn't stop print finishers the world over from trying to score heavy stock with the rotary scoring devices on their folding machines – usually at the request of a frantic production manager who hadn't scheduled pre-creasing into the job. Consequently, the folding-machine operator would spend hours tweaking the set up and process trying to produce a score that didn't crack on the fold. But such last-ditch efforts failed 80 to 85 per cent of the time. And the shortcomings were costly and time consuming.

Not even the most skilled print finishers were able to adequately reduce, much less eliminate, the cracking caused by rotary scoring tools. The only way to avoid cracking was to run the printed sheets through an off-line flatbed creasing platen. A few of the large printing and print-finishing companies had their own platen machines, but even then, pre-creasing significantly slowed production because the platens don't usually exceed 2,000 sheets per hour while folding machines average something in the region of 15,000-20,000 sheets per hour. Most printing and print-finishing companies did not even have platen machines, which were expensive, viewed as "old school," and highly specialized – requiring expertise beyond that of most operators. So for the vast majority of printing and print-finishing shops, the only way to avoid cracking was to outsource the pre-creasing – at considerable expense.

The company where I was working at the time was spending more than £50,000 a year on pre-crease outsourcing – plus the additional cost of resulting production delays. Sometimes, we had to shut down the entire finishing process while we waited for covers to be creased. Having to send dozens of pallets of sheets across town for pre-creasing, sometimes on a daily basis, and waiting days for them to return so we could trim and fold was not only expensive, it was also frustrating. Not just that, handing over control of the creasing might also cause us to miss deadlines or compromise quality, which could have made the high cost of outsourcing seem like a secondary issue.

The print-finishing fraternity rarely spoke about this problem. It was the great challenge that would remain nameless – the elephant in the room. But there's no doubt whatsoever that, if we all could have had one request granted to improve our working lives, it would have been to have the ability to score heavier stocks on folding machines using a rotary device that didn't cause cracking. Among the hundreds of thousands of people involved in print production, though, it went without saying that it was categorically impossible for a rotary scoring device *not* to cause cracking. It was such a given that none of the folding-machine manufacturers had ever produced such a tool, and if word had got out that someone was trying to create a rotary scoring device that eliminated cracking, that person would have been deemed delusional.

But what if someone did?

What would such a groundbreaking invention be worth to print-finishing departments and companies? I couldn't help but entertain that possibility.

I estimated that at least 10,000 of the 14,000 print-production companies in the United Kingdom, each spent at least £15,000 a year on pre-crease outsourcing – which worked out to £150 million in the U.K. alone. And that was a conservative estimate. Then, when you extend that number worldwide, that number became huge. I also considered the additional cost of production delays incurred by pre-creasing, especially if it had to be outsourced. I could only guess at the total potential savings to printing and print-finishing companies worldwide. I figured that if anyone came up with a solution that allowed print finishers to perfectly crease and fold heavier stocks on their folding machines, that person would probably be a millionaire!

Despite the odds, I decided to tackle this problem. But I wasn't so naïve as to think I could eliminate cracking. My initial intention was to create a solution that *reduced* cracking enough to allow printing companies to keep significantly more of their work in-house. That seemed like a realistic compromise.

I also decided to take on this enormous challenge single-handedly, without consulting any of my colleagues or the equipment reps I'd dealt with. For one thing, they would have laughed in my face. More importantly, I knew better than to confide in anyone. I'd nearly lost my job a few years earlier after a co-worker with whom I'd shared my plan to start a business told my boss, and I wasn't about to make that mistake again.

Recalling that experience also reminded me of the half dozen or so times I'd tried to pass along my ideas for improving a piece of equipment to a manufacturer's sales rep or technician. Nothing had ever come of it. Suddenly, it dawned on me why: They weren't interested in just an *idea*. An idea is no more useful than an empty dream. It's only when an idea is brought to life, when it can be examined and its value demonstrated, that it has the potential to open doors.

It then occurred to me that the reps' lack of interest in my ideas might also have been due to my lowly position in the pecking order. They would have thought me, a mere print finisher at the time, incapable of coming up with a useful, bankable innovation. Even the most gifted print finishers are usually the lowest paid and least respected workers in the print-production hierarchy.

But I desperately wanted to be taken more seriously – and to ditch my green print-finisher's T-shirt for a business suit. Solving the cracking on the fold caused by rotary scoring devices would make that possible. So that was the problem I decided to solve, driven by my fear of being stuck in a middle-management job for the rest of my working life.

> *"You are just as likely to solve a problem by being unconventional and determined as by being brilliant."* — James Dyson

A Mad Search For A Solution

From the moment I settled on tackling the cracking issue, I knew the solution had to be a rotary scoring tool that would fit on a standard folding machine and could consistently produce a clean score on any type of paper stock.

I gave myself six months to figure out how to do that, build a prototype, and sell my idea. I considered taking out a £2,000 bank loan to fund my new venture, but decided to ask my sister instead. I offered to repay £2,000 plus £500 by way of a reward for her kindness within six months, and thankfully, she agreed. Her generous backing was enough to get me started. And while Sue was slightly concerned, she backed me all the same.

Then I did something that most people might consider crazy: I asked my boss if I could use the company's folding machines after my shift to test something I was developing on my own time. Given the hard lesson I'd learned when my old boss had caught wind of my previous venture, I wanted to be upfront this time but not divulge too much too soon. So I told my boss, Keith, about my hope of designing a better scoring tool, one that would save his company a lot of money, and selling it to a manufacturer. To my surprise, Keith agreed to let me test my device on the company's equipment after I clocked out, although I'm quite certain he thought nothing would come of my lofty plan.

I threw myself into this exciting project with a level of commitment and purpose unlike anything I'd experienced before. I'd never worked so hard, mentally or physically, in my life. That is saying something, considering I had always poured my heart and soul into my work, particularly in a technical and creative sense.

All rotary scoring tools at the time consisted of two circular steel collars – one that fit onto the upper shaft and one that fit onto the lower shaft of a folding machine. As each sheet of paper moved through the rotating top and bottom shafts, a slightly protruding metal rim, called a *blade*, on the upper *male* collar pressed the paper into a corresponding metal channel on the lower *female* collar. This created a V-shaped indentation, or *score*, where the paper would be folded.

By that time in my career, I had used, at one time or another, all of the rotary scoring tools in existence – including the few that had been designed to reduce cracking. Those devices had failed time and time again, and many ended up gathering dust on the shelves of the back wall. I'd also applied all of the tricks of the trade that print finishers everywhere had tried to reduce cracking. I worked hours and hours after my day job, studying those methods, replicating them, and putting my own spin on them.

During my many years as a print finisher, I'd found that scoring into rubber on the lower collar, which I'd have to jimmy-rig, reduced cracking somewhat. A couple of machine manufacturers had already developed rotary scoring tools with similar rubber collars. So I knew I categorically needed to use rubber to soften the scoring application; steel was simply too harsh. The technique I'd used took extra time and technical expertise, and it brought only a 15 to 20 per cent success rate – which was admittedly better than the all-metal collars but wasn't nearly good enough. I figured that if I could create a rotary scoring device that eliminated cracking 40 to 50 per cent of the time, then I might be on to something. I even went so far as to envision inventing a rotary scoring device that created a flatbed-quality crease on heavy stock 100 per cent of the time – but that was just wishful thinking.

I started by putting together a sketch of the lower collar of a rotary scoring device with a channel encircling it, into which two O-rings would be sunk. My idea was to run the metal blade of an existing male collar between the O-rings on my prototype. For that purpose, I'd secured sample O-rings from a specialized rubber components manufacturer. Coincidentally, I'd learned of the company from a printing equipment manufacturer's rep who had dropped by my place of employment a couple of weeks prior and raved about how a rubber washer had improved one of his products. Knowing I would need rubber for my device, I'd taken note of the rubber supplier's telephone number and called them a few days later.

On my lunch break, I excitedly strolled over to an engineering firm across the road, introduced myself, and explained the basics of my project and what I wanted to achieve. As I would soon learn, they were accustomed to customers coming in for scheduled appointments wearing suits and handing over professionally engineering drawings. There I was, in my work trousers and T-shirt, with a hand-drawn sketch on a sheet of regular unlined paper. I immediately sensed that this company would not take me seriously. Nevertheless, they agreed to produce what they thought I needed, based on my rough drawings.

Although it seemed to irk the firm's manager, I coached the engineer through each stage of prototyping, helping him to interpret my drawings. The engineer was able to easily fabricate the steel collar on his lathe using the measurements I had provided. However, getting the width of the channel correct proved to be more difficult. It took several tries to get it right and before a test run produced good results.

In fact, my prototype worked better than the Super-Score™ tool (by MBO, a leading global print-equipment manufacturer) that I had tried some years before. The Super-Score had a steel blade that scored into a polyurethane bed, which admittedly did improve the look of the score. Its downside was that the polyurethane section wore quickly and was expensive to replace. My device was a potential improvement on two levels because the result was better and the O-rings would be faster and cheaper to replace.

At that point, I started to worry about being copied, so I did an Internet search for patents that had been taken out to protect similar assemblies. My heart sank when I found plenty of *prior art* describing similar inventions, but none had been granted patents or had patents pending (yet), which made me feel better. Although

I was encouraged that I might have something I could use legally, I remained concerned that I would be unable to patent my idea – which would of course leave the door wide open for someone to copy it. I'd recently read about such horrors in James Dyson's book about inventing his Dual Cyclone vacuum cleaner, and how he dealt with those only too willing to exploit his own ideas.

After making a few more adjustments to my design, I again put it to the test. I slipped my latest prototype onto the bottom shaft of the folding machine, loaded some medium-weight stock onto the feeder, and ran several sheets through the machine at high speed. The steel blade pressed into the rubber bed with no problem and produced a more defined score than existing rotary scoring tools – even Heidelberg's. Further testing showed that my device would also score medium to heavy stock with no cracking 20 to 25 per cent of the time. Although this was 5 to 10 per cent better than using a rotary scoring device with a polyurethane bed, it would be difficult to sell because it didn't improve results enough. The results would be unpredictable too; operators would have to rely on trial and error to determine which stocks did and did not work.

I asked myself: *Is this good enough?*

The answer, I admitted with great disappointment, was, *No*. But I was not ready or willing to give up the fight quite yet.

Eureka! ... Now What?

That evening, after my latest prototype failed to produce a good-enough result, I dug deep and tapped into my self-belief and faith, hoping that I might persevere and make a breakthrough.

This was one of those defining moments in my business journey that I will never forget. Sue and I had recently attended a Christianity course at our local church and one night at home, for the first time, I began to pray on my own for some kind of resolution to this problem I desperately wanted to solve. At first this felt strange and uncomfortable, and then it was like something changed. I found renewed inspiration and a greater sense of passion.

It would have been easy to leave this part of my story out of my book, not least because I know how some people have reacted when I mention it. But it would have been wrong to ignore it; I feel it is pivotal in terms of how our journey continued and our faith strengthened. Sue and I love our business, but we also feel privileged to be in the position to be able to support local and international charities. Furthermore, it felt amazing, in 2015, when we were able to set up a separate charity account to fund this work. Sue and I are private people, however, and we both feel that the success of our business has given us the opportunity to make a difference to people's lives, and this is a big part of what drives us forward.

So, in return, I promised to use a portion of whatever profit my device might bring to help our church and the people in our community. There were now two incentives. As I prayed, I felt my initial dejection slip away and my confidence return.

The following Tuesday after finishing my shift, I went back to work on my prototype, determined to find a way to improve it. But I'd tried everything I could think of, and I was deeply disappointed that I'd come up short. In frustration, I yanked at one of the O-rings to remove it, which caused it to roll out of the channel in which it was embedded and into the shallower vacant channel next to it.

I looked at the wayward O-ring, which protruded halfway out of the channel – much like, I realized, the metal blade on the upper collar of a standard rotary scoring tool. Purely out of curiosity, I attached my makeshift rubber-bladed collar to the upper shaft of my folding machine and ran it in a grooved collar on the lower shaft. As I loaded some medium-weight stock and pushed the start button, I thought, *How stupid, imagine using rubber as the male scoring component...*

To my amazement, my "stupid" contraption produced a nice, crisp crease!

Continuing my playful experiment, I ran some heavy stock through my machine at slow speed and watched a few sheets pass through my rather precarious O-ring assembly. What I witnessed next utterly astounded me: a crease as deep and wide as the ones produced with flatbed platen machines! Not only that, but upon closer inspection I saw that my makeshift device had produced the same *U-shaped bead* that flatbed platens created, rather than the *V-shaped indentation* created by existing rotary scoring tools!

I hand-folded the piece of blue card stock. There was no sign of cracking whatsoever. A metal score would have damaged the fibres or ripped the material in half, even if I had run it into my double O-ring bed. The softer contact offered by the rubber composition was the key.

My heart skipped a beat and a shudder ran down my spine. I had to step back as I realized the enormity of what I had: In attempting to develop a rotary *scoring* device that would *reduce* cracking, I had potentially created the world's first rotary *creasing* device, which might *eliminate* cracking altogether.

That Eureka moment filled me with euphoria. Looking at my simple O-ring assembly, I nearly laughed out loud at the absurdity of my rather basic and comical-looking device being the culmination of twenty years of creative thinking and self-taught methodologies. Surely the Big Idea that could potentially solve a multi-billion-dollar problem in the world of print finishing and change my life should be more sophisticated? What irony, I thought with amusement, that a common O-ring, a common part typically used as a seal or pulley in thousands of products, including Dyson's revolutionary Dual-Cyclone vacuum cleaner, was the pivotal component of my invention.

My elation was soon replaced with self-doubt...

Suddenly, my idea seemed too simple and obvious not to have been tried by others. I wondered whether someone else had attempted the concept but abandoned it due to some fatal flaw that I had yet to uncover. Even if that were not the case, I had no clue how to get my invention to the next level, and I worried that my idea was too big for me, and that maybe I should hand it over to someone else.

But then I thought, *Why not me? If I could get this far on my own, I can figure out how to perfect my invention and then sell it to Heidelberg or another big print-equipment manufacturer.*

When I made my big breakthrough, I was alone in a room with two or three print workers on the late shift. In my excitement, I was tempted to tell them about my incredible discovery. But without a patent, that would have been risky and reckless. The initial, quick payoff derived from announcing my great news would have soon been overwhelmed by worry that my idea might suddenly go viral, bringing in early competition before I even got to the next phase. On a legal and technical level, I also knew from having researched the patent process that disclosing any information regarding my invention could end up invalidating my future patents. So I resolved to shut out the outside world until I got my final design sorted out and had registered my patent.

I'd never kept a personal journal or any record of my work, instead relying on my memory to keep track of everything I'd learned about print finishing. The incident with the runaway O-ring changed that; I knew I needed to somehow document this extraordinary event. A few days later I purchased my first diary to log the important details relating to my thought processes and the facts surrounding my discovery. (Little did I know that years later my diary would be used as evidence in a litigation case).

In my newly acquired logbook, I registered January 12, 1999, as the day my invention was born – less than three weeks after I'd decided to tackle the cracking problem caused by rotary scoring tools. That left about five months of my self-imposed six-month deadline to refine, test and sell my idea. I had a long way to go. So I pressed forward with even more vigour and passion.

I not only wanted my device to consistently produce a superior crease on all common types of stock, but I also wanted it to be easy to set up and use. The depth and width of the crease would need to vary, depending on the thickness and stiffness of the paper and the material used to coat it. So I decided to create a set of predetermined settings for each weight of stock – light, medium, and heavy.

It took an immense amount of work to determine the correct shape, height, and width of the rubber blade in the upper collar as well as the correct corresponding width and depth of the metal channel in the lower collar for each setting. One of the directors at the rubber company, John McNorton, who had taken me under his wing, directed me to several O-rings he thought might work. The depth of the protruding rubber was critical to the strength of the crease, so I wanted to provide two depths for each type of stock. That way, if the user found the crease to be a little weak, he could pry it out of the deeper channel and roll it into the shallower channel for that stock type to produce a stronger crease. I kept the engineering shop across the street busy machining channels of varying dimensions into the metal surface of the female collar.

After considerable trial and error and testing on numerous stocks, I arrived at the best configurations for medium and heavy stocks. But none of the O-rings I'd tried had produced the desired results on lighter paper. After discussing this with John McNorton, he worked with me to produce a flatter, washer-shaped insert that was slightly narrower than the O-rings I'd tried previously. Although the insert was fiddly to put into the channel, it produced very good results on paper stocks.

Once I'd nailed down all six creasing settings (two depths for each of the three types of stock), the engineering shop produced two prototypes and a complete set of drawings. The first thing I did was visit a patent attorney. I chose Serjeants in the city of Leicester because it was local and in the middle price range. I'd already spent almost half of the £2,000 I'd borrowed from my sister on my prototypes. The bulk of the remaining money was used to help pay for my U.K. patent application; the rest would go to future refinements to my prototypes.

As I was waiting for my patent registration number to come through so I could tell the world about my invention, I was hit by a blow that threatened everything I had worked so hard for. During the testing of some heavy stock, the rubber began to perish; it seemed to simply burn away. I chastised myself: *This is probably why I haven't seen rubber used to crease card stock before - because it wears out so fast.*

My spirits a little low, I again visited John McNorton to see whether he had any ideas on how to solve the problem. John smiled and said he would mix a heat-resistant formula for me to try - something he was sure wouldn't burn out. He was right; subsequent testing proved the new rubber to be successful.

At that point, I hadn't run more than 1,000 sheets at a time, and I needed to do bigger tests to see how my device performed when creasing the standard production run of 10,000 or more sheets. My plan was to give my boss, Keith, an update on my invention and ask him if I could use my prototypes to crease some live jobs in his factory. As eager as I was to press forward, however, I dared not reveal anything about my idea until my patent registration number came through because doing so could prevent me from being granted a patent. Meanwhile, I was like a racehorse champing at the bit, raring to go.

Chapter 3

Like a Red Rag to a Bull

TWENTY YEARS of hard work, continually striving to devise solutions to the challenges of my trade, had finally reached a crucial tipping point. Driven by my fear of being average and the undeniably magnetic attraction of being my own boss, I'd arrived at a key moment having invented a device that had the potential to transform an industry *and* my life.

That possibility was thrilling – and a bit terrifying at the same time. If my device worked as well in real life as it had in my small test runs, I figured that surely one of the big print-equipment manufacturers might pay a good price for exclusive rights to my invention. But that was a big *if*.

Producing a few hundred perfectly creased scrap sheets in my spare time was a different ball game in comparison to consistently producing tens of thousands of perfectly creased sheets at a time for paying clients.

Besides, I still hadn't even asked my boss's permission to test my device on an actual live job. *What if he said no?*

How else could I prove that my device worked well on a standard run of 10,000 or more sheets?

What if he said yes and my device failed to produce a crease that stopped the folds from cracking, time after time?

What if my rotary creaser performed brilliantly but my boss took offence to my ambitions and showed me the door before I could sell my idea?

How would I support my family and fund the further development and marketing of my device?

When I allowed those thoughts to crowd my mind one after another, my confidence would falter. But then, as a motivational counter-balance, I'd picture the grey-haired version of myself still working in someone else's business, and I'd dig in my heels and push onward.

One thing I did to preserve momentum while waiting to receive my patent-pending status was to plan out and practice what I'd say when I could finally present my invention to the world. As I rehearsed my product demonstration, I would imagine how excited Heidelberg and other industry leaders would be to see the first rotary creasing device to *eliminate* cracking on their folding machines!

Dismissal And Disbelief

A few days after submitting my patent application, an equipment sales representative visited the shop where I was employed, Streamline Press. We had purchased most of our finishing machines from this person, and over the years I had developed a good rapport with him. As we were finishing up our usual business chat, I decided to tell him about my invention, thinking he might be willing to help me set up a demonstration with his employer, MBO, one of the top print-equipment manufacturers in the world.

When I told the MBO rep I had a rotary-creasing solution I wanted to show him once I could officially divulge the details, his eyes lit up. But instead of offering to take my device straight to MBO, he told me about a customer of his that was about to buy a £10,000 offline creasing cylinder to process some book covers they'd been struggling to score on their folding machines and asked if I would try to help them out.

I had a potential customer. All I had to do was call the client – Polestar, in Bradford – to schedule a demonstration. Without hesitation, I excitedly assured him I would do just that.

Having that challenge and purpose inspired me, and before I had a chance to think about it, I found myself in my boss's office seeking his permission to test my device on a "live" job to make certain it was up to the task. As an incentive, I showed Keith the flawless spines I'd produced during my after-hours tests, and thankfully he gave me the okay to put my prototypes to work on live jobs.

That same afternoon, two pallets of unfolded mailers that normally would have been sent out for creasing on a special platen machine were held back for me to test in secret. I had to make sure no other person was present; I couldn't disclose any details about my device due to the risk of invalidating my patent. Quite nervously I watched as the mailers, which had been printed on a dark-coloured, heavy stock, passed through the folding machine. All 50,000 sheets creased and folded immaculately. It was the first time ever I had witnessed such stock running through a folding machine with no cracking on the fold. What's more, the rubber component of my creasing device showed no sign of wear whatsoever – I was elated and couldn't sleep that night.

A few days later, my patent-pending status arrived, and I again went to see my boss. Wanting to be honest and to exercise some of those Christian values I'd been learning about, I explained to Keith that the testing had gone better than I had hoped and I was investigating a business idea.

A look of surprise flashed across his face.

I held my breath during the few seconds it took Keith to respond, my mind racing. *Did I really just say that?*

Was I asking to be fired, telling my boss I might leave his company if my idea panned out?

Was I crazy putting my job on the line when I had a wife and two young children to support?

What Keith said next motivated me as much as anything I've ever heard.

"Graham, your creasing device will never make you anything more than pin money. You should sell your prototypes to Heidelberg for a few thousand quid or whatever you can get, and take your family on holiday."

As if that wasn't disparaging enough, Keith had more to say. "You have the best job you will ever have working for me. If you leave, you will struggle to get another job as good."

His words were like a red rag to a bull.

But they completely backfired. Rather than discouraging me, Keith's dismissal actively propelled me forward with my plan to leave his company and strike out on my own.

Don't get me wrong; Keith was a great boss, and I really did like and respect him. But he was guilty of what many people in authority, or who think they're in authority, do: He placed me in a box with a label on it, sizing me up and putting a limit on what I could accomplish.

I got the feeling that Keith thought I would take his advice. But instead of knocking me down, his stinging remarks fired me up and pushed me forward. And I immediately booked an appointment with the print manager at the Polestar division in Bradford, England.

In the days leading up to my appointment with Polestar, I was again hit with the feeling that my invention might be a bit too hot for me to handle. *Maybe Keith is right*, I thought. *Maybe I should hand it over to Heidelberg or MBO or whichever manufacturer would be willing to pay whatever sum for it.*

Those, after all, had been my thoughts immediately after my Eureka moment, when I'd realized the enormous potential of my simple invention. At the time, I'd researched potential buyers for my invention – specifically, folding-machine manufacturers. Today, inventors can use the Internet to learn almost everything they need to know about potential buyers, licensors, and other business partners. Back then; I'd had to use other means to get that information. Thanks to my work experience and my habit of reading trade magazines, I had a good idea of which companies to approach. I also had working relationships with some of their sales reps and technicians. I'd tapped into those resources to find the names and contact information of product managers within those organizations.

So, when those feelings of insecurity came back just before my visit to Polestar, I contacted all of the leading folding-machine manufacturers. Not one of them would give me the time of day, and only one, the product manager at Heidelberg, offered any explanation why he'd turned me down. I'll never forget his words.

With hope in my heart, I introduced myself as the inventor of a new rotary creasing device that eliminated the major problem of cracking on folding machines. I went on to speak of the benefits my breakthrough product would allow Heidelberg to offer its customers. Then, I enthusiastically invited him to come to the U.K.

to see it for himself.

He turned me down flat. He told me he received calls weekly from people like me claiming to have the next great solution, and he had no intention of wasting his time visiting me. To add insult to injury, he ended the call by saying his company had a department of more than a thousand people working on new ideas all the time, and if the problem I claimed to have solved could be solved, then one of them would have already done so.

Although I was surprised and disappointed at being summarily dismissed by the big guns of my industry, I wasted little time licking my wounds. Indeed, I took satisfaction in knowing that I had accomplished what a thousand R&D guys at the largest print-equipment manufacturing firm in the world had failed to do. There and then, I chose to turn rejection into opportunity. I'd just have to do things differently than I'd originally planned.

I'd begin, I decided, by canvassing print-finishing outfits within a two-hour driving distance from our home.

I set the price of my rotary creasing tool at £359 apiece. My pricing strategy was simple (too simple, I'd later learn): I merely doubled the cost of the steel rotary scoring devices that came with folding machines. At the time, it seemed like a good starting price, based on knowing how much money my device could potentially save customers and estimating how much they'd be willing to pay for it.

Of course, the proof was in the pudding. This was a big deal for me and I prayed that my device would work its magic at Polestar.

The day of my appointment, I took an early shift

so I could leave at 1:30 pm. I had an old Ford Cortina, which I parked behind Polestar's building so no one inside could see it. I was dressed smartly enough, though not in a suit, and I had a plan in mind. If all went well, Polestar would purchase both of my prototypes for £359 apiece. My wife, Sue, who was beginning to help me organise the business, advised me to ask for the full purchase price upfront, because we needed the money to pay for more devices and for patent costs.

The print manager, Vic Furness, immediately put me at ease. He began by saying that I was his last hope but he would understand if my device didn't solve his cracking problem. Nothing else they'd tried had worked, so if my device did the trick, great, but if not, they'd have to spend £10,000 for a large platen machine.

Vic took me to the finishing department, where an operator showed me a bunch of book covers that were splitting open on the spine. As I removed the steel scoring tools that were wreaking the havoc and replaced them with my prototypes, I couldn't help but notice the dubious look on the operator's face. Within two minutes, though, his expression changed to amazement as he watched the strange-looking O-ring gadgets working their miracle. Soon, the operator on the next machine gathered around, as did the guillotine operator, the forklift driver, a few office staff and probably the warehouse cat. I was pushed farther and farther to the outside of the ever-increasing circle. It wasn't me who was the star; it was my creasing device.

In fact, I didn't need to say much more. I advised on some simple set-up procedures, and my job was done. I didn't even have to try to sell my device, much less ask for payment upfront. Vic got his chequebook and paid for the two prototypes on the spot.

My first product demonstration could not have gone better. I sang with joy all the way home.

Grabbing The Bull By The Horns

Selling my two prototypes to Polestar gave me the confidence and courage I needed to push forward with my wide-eyed scheme to parlay my funny-looking invention into a profitable business.

I figured that 10,000 of the 14,000 companies with print finishing operations in the United Kingdom would benefit from my solution. Knowing it was unrealistic to expect all 10,000 of those firms to purchase my device, I aimed at an initial target of 1,000 and estimated that each of those companies would purchase at least two devices. Then I began to think of the global market. The United States, alone, had up to 60,000 potential buyers of my solution!

Before I could get too carried away with my wishful calculations, the realities of life brought me back down to earth. I'd have to sell a whole lot more than two devices to get my business off the ground and doing well enough that I could quit my factory job.

My instincts told me that what I needed most was to generate some customer leads. Without some kind of sales volume, or at least a hope of sales, the business wouldn't get off the ground. As a long-time subscriber to print-industry magazines, I'd read countless articles about new businesses and new business deals. I also recalled how fascinated I'd been by Fireman Mick's story of his friend being offered half a million pounds for his invention. I figured that if I could convince *Printweek*, the U.K.'s leading magazine for the print trade, to write a story about the first sale of my new creasing device, perhaps that would generate some interest in my product.

First, I checked with Vic Furness, the product manager at Polestar, to see whether he'd be willing to talk to a reporter. Vic was delighted to oblige. Then, I called the editor at *Printweek*, who took an immediate interest in my story and set me up with one of her reporters.

The reporter, Gordon Carson, interviewed me by phone. I told Gordon my "poor lowly inventor's story": how I had come up with something potentially ground-breaking but was struggling to attract attention from investors and manufacturers, so I'd been forced to bring it to market myself. I told him how, within days of receiving my patent-pending notification, I'd landed my first product demonstration, which had brought my first sale and with it my first satisfied customer. Gordon lapped it up. He assured me he'd contact Vic Furness and include his remarks in the article, which would appear in the next issue of *Printweek*.

"Get someone else to blow your horn, and the sound will carry twice as far." — Will Rogers

A couple of weeks before the article came out, I had a long discussion with my wife, Sue, about how my business idea might evolve. I'd previously shared with Sue how well my device had worked for my employer, Streamline Press, and how much money in outsourced creasing costs it could potentially save them. In my mind, the quick and easy sale to Polestar, a £718 purchase that had saved them more than £9,000 by not having to buy a platen, further validated the value and need for my device. I convinced Sue that there were many other companies like Polestar, and I would find them.

Sue knew how unhappy I was at work and how passionate I was about starting a business. She'd allowed me to work toward making that dream a reality, and she was willing to contribute her talents toward that effort. But we had two young children to think about and a mortgage to pay. We really didn't know how successful this new venture might be. We decided we couldn't gamble on me giving up my day job after only one successful sale. So we agreed to carry on with this venture as sort of a sideline hobby and to see where it might lead. Then, we worked out a plan to start marketing and selling my device.

First, we needed to name the product. After we'd brainstormed a few names that didn't quite hit the mark, I described my creasing device to Sue in greater detail, emphasizing why it needed three settings. Then Sue came up with her first moment of genius as far as the business was concerned . . .

"Tri-Creaser," she casually suggested.

Tri-Creaser! It was perfect!

We also decided that we needed a promotional leaflet for prospects and a user's guide for customers. We created the user's guide ourselves. Since we didn't own a computer and desktop printer at the time, I dictated while Sue typed up the set-up and operation instructions. We made photocopies of the user's guide to give to customers.

I enlisted the help of a friend who worked at a local print shop to help me design the leaflet, which included photographs and a description of the Tri-Creaser as well as contact information. In writing the leaflet, I tried to put myself in the customers' shoes, citing the product details they'd want to know and explaining how the device would benefit them. We paid a nominal amount for the leaflets, using some of the funds from the Polestar sale. I also acquired some generic packaging and did my best to make it look decent.

As a result of a bit of DIY ingenuity, everything was in place to follow up on the leads I hoped the *Printweek* editorial would bring. I thought about what I'd say to callers and practiced my product demonstration.

Then, on the Sunday evening before the *Printweek* issue bearing my story would be delivered to over 12,000 printing companies in the U.K., including the company for which I worked, I began to worry. *Had my heart-to-heart with Keith given me the license to set this in motion? Of course it hadn't! Surely, I had taken this too far . . .*

The thought of my boss reading the latest progress report on my new business in *Printweek* horrified me. To prevent that from happening, I had no choice but to intercept Streamline's copies of the magazine the next morning. Despite my angst, the absurdity of the situation made me smile.

The next day at work, just before 9:00 am, I followed the postman upstairs. Fortunately, not all of the office staff had arrived, and no one else was in the mailroom. So I waited until the postman left before shoving the two copies of *Printweek* up my T-shirt and hurrying downstairs. I found a safe place in the dispatch area to read the article.

Shivers ran up my spine as I flicked through the pages to find my story. Titled "Innovative Solution to Printers' Creasing Hassles," it was well placed at the top of an early right-hand page. Gordon had written a compelling article and included my home phone number that appeared at the end. All morning, I wondered whether anyone would even call. Knowing no one would be home to answer the phone, as Sue worked Mondays, I'd made sure the answering machine was operational and turned on before leaving for work that morning.

After my shift ended, I rushed home to check for voice messages. The phone was ringing as I entered the house. It was a printing company wanting to know more about my creasing device – and I'd made it there just in time to book an appointment to demonstrate it. As soon as I put the receiver back in the cradle, the phone rang again with another inquiry about the Tri-Creaser. This continued for the next three hours, until 6:00 pm, by which time I'd written down the names and contact information of 25 separate printing companies that were interested in knowing more about my device.

…Then, I played back the voice messages: another 40 inquiries. I was astounded. Although it was what I'd hoped for, I wasn't really prepared for it.

Later that evening when I told Sue of the remarkable response, she was a little taken aback. Frankly, I was as surprised as she was, and obviously we were both excited.

Sue offered to stay home on Tuesday to answer the phone, but I figured the next day would be quieter, and I didn't want Sue to have to take time off work needlessly. To my astonishment, the next day brought just as many calls. Again, I spent the afternoon answering the phone and expanding my list of prospects. And when the phone finally stopped ringing, I listened to one message after another on the answering machine.

Unfortunately, the tape malfunctioned after around 20 messages, but, astonishingly, in just two days, I had a list of more than 100 contacts. That's what you call a good response to a press article.

Every day that week, I rushed home after clocking out and spent the afternoon returning calls. Altogether, I set up 38 demonstrations within a week following the publication of the *Printweek* article. Most of the other callers for which a demo was not set up requested prices and more information, and I sent them my jazzy leaflet and a personalized cover letter.

I scheduled the first product demonstrations a week out to allow time to have 30 more devices made, using the proceeds from the sale to Polestar to pay for them. On days I had a product demonstration, I'd clock off work at 1:30 pm and travel to the prospective customer's site. I sometimes had to take a day or two off work to visit a customer site that was farther away.

I always brought along a few packaged Tri-Creasers to sell on the spot, hoping things would go as they had at Polestar. They usually did. Time after time, I'd be met with the same scepticism upon hearing my claims — closely followed by shock or amusement when they first laid eyes on my strange O-ring device, followed by amazement at seeing the Tri-Creaser actually work its magic, followed by a cheque being placed in hand. Every few weeks, I'd have more devices made, again using some of the proceeds from the Tri-Creaser sales. Within a few months, I'd repaid the debt to my sister, well ahead of my six-month goal.

At first I made a point of dressing smart enough to impress but in practical clothing that allowed me to install the Tri-Creasers myself, as that involved getting my hands dirty. I quickly learned that each company I visited had operators on hand to do the installing, and all I had to do was coach them through it. So I began wearing a suit and tie, as I wanted to come across as more professional in the managing director's or owner's office. Sometimes, the sale involved a bit of negotiating, and I became well practiced in that discipline. I also improved the user's guide so that my verbal prompts to the operators were minimal and I could focus on facilitating what was typically a remarkably easy sale.

To drum up additional product demos, I reached out to former co-workers who had landed jobs at other firms in my city, and they helped me get into those companies.

Everywhere I went, my Tri-Creaser delivered exactly what I promised. Customers wanted my solution, and I had no competition. But having to travel to customer sites after my day job meant I could sell only a few devices a week.

> *"Things may come to those who wait, but only things left by those who hustle."*
> — Abraham Lincoln

Taking The Leap

Six months into my "side-line" business, I was extraordinarily busy demonstrating and selling Tri-Creasers, and my confidence was soaring. Each device cost us about £25 to produce, and Sue had worked out the other costs, for the marketing leaflet, user's guide, packaging, travel, and administration. The profit margin looked amazingly healthy at a touch over £300 per device. I'd set a goal of selling 100 Tri-Creasers within the first year, which would bring an annual profit that far exceeded what I was earning in my day job. But still, I was too afraid to break out of the safety zone of a guaranteed pay cheque to pursue my new venture full-time.

Instead, I went to my boss, Keith, and informed him of my conflict of interest, explaining that with the success of my business, my enthusiasm and desire to remain as his print-finishing manager had diminished. I then boldly suggested I could continue giving him 100 per cent in a demoted position, working on his machines. Although Keith agreed to employ me in this reduced capacity and at a reduced wage, he still took pleasure in telling me that I was making a huge mistake. Apparently, he still had no confidence in my abilities.

At about that time, Sue hatched a plan to sell the Tri-Creaser through direct mail. This was an example of her fantastic business brain at work. We thought that sales would increase and the cost-per-sale would decrease if I didn't have to rely solely on me traveling all over the U.K. to demonstrate, sell, and install my products. After all, I had gone to great lengths to design my rotary creasing device to be much easier to install than the steel scoring devices supplied with folding machines. After six months of seeing how easily operators could set up and use the Tri-Creaser with the instruction sheet we provided and minimal instruction from me, I felt confident I didn't need to be there.

To ensure that operators could install the Tri-Creaser on their own, I again made improvements to the user guide. At the same time, we also upgraded the packaging to improve both the aesthetics and durability of the container that the product went out in. Steadily, piece-by-piece, I was improving both the product and its backup.

As with face-to-face sales, we asked for the cheque upfront – which no one else in our industry would dare contemplate requesting. But at this vital stage of our fledgling operation we needed cash flow, not money owed, and in the end most customers came around without too much fuss. Although some prospects still required an on-site product demonstration, our new business model worked remarkably well for an increasing percentage of our business. Sue and I were at the post office every night, sometimes sending out four to seven Tri-Creasers at a time, all over the U.K. Sales went up and so did profits. I have no hesitation in saying that the mail order program/cash up-front combination was a stroke of genius on Sue's behalf and it was making us cash rich in the process. Soon I was earning much more than what I was being paid at Streamline.

Meanwhile, I never gave less than my best to my day job at Streamline, but it was agony. My heart wasn't in it, and my mind was quite understandably focused on my afternoon adventures.

Finally, twelve months after taking my product to market myself, I decided to hand in my notice at Streamline. Sue gave me her blessings – though I could tell the thought of me giving up my good job was tough on her. She really had no idea of the potential market for my invention and just had to take my word for it.

On my last day at Streamline, the print manager shuffled over for a word. He told me Keith wanted to buy two Tri-Creasers and wondered if I could sort out a discount.

There was no hesitation in my response. "I am running a business, not a charity. He will have to pay the full price."

It was my way of letting Keith know I was serious about my future and that I knew full well that my device was worth more than his idea of "pin money." I would like to think Keith respected me for that – and it felt great being handed over a cheque for £718. I could not have asked for a better farewell present.

Within a week of leaving Streamline, my Tri-Creaser sales tripled. Why hadn't I quit my job months before? In retrospect, I realise that I hadn't been confident enough before then to take the risk. But when I finally did take that leap of faith, I threw myself into my business with even more passion and determination.

One of the first things I did was to increase the unit price of the Tri-Creaser – a decision that came about as much from my own insecurity as from good business sense. At the time, my customer-service strategy consisted of ringing up each new customer a few weeks after the sale to inquire how they were getting on – half expecting them to tell me the device wasn't working properly or the rubber component had burned out. Instead, almost all of my customers raved about the Tri-Creaser, and many told me it had paid for itself within a couple of weeks. After hearing that time and again, I raised the price from £359 to £395 per device.

At the same time, I began to develop additional models of the Tri-Creaser. Initially, I'd created two versions to fit the most popular types of folding machines. Each of the two leading folding-machine manufacturers, Heidelberg and MBO, produced at least three types of machines, for which I'd determined early on I'd need four different sizes of my device. The need for additional sizes was driven home when several of the companies that had seen the *Printweek* article called months later to inquire whether I had a rotary creasing device for the types of folding machines they used. Within two months of leaving my day job, I had developed the two additional and refined the two existing Tri-Creaser models to provide the four sizes needed for the most popular types of folding machines.

By the end of my first year in business, I'd sold over 200 Tri-Creasers – double my original goal. The time was right for Sue to come on board full-time.

David And Goliaths

During that first year of peddling Tri-Creasers to U.K. print companies in my spare time, I repeatedly witnessed the elation on customers' faces when they saw my device transform the quality of their finished work. Again and again, customers expressed their amazement at how much time, effort, and money the Tri-Creaser was saving them. But I desperately wanted to make my device available to print finishers around the world – sooner rather than later, before someone copied my idea. There seemed to be two obvious ways to do this. Selling my invention outright was an option and would represent a quick but possibly unsatisfying payoff. The alternative option involved getting a reseller or licensing deal with a major manufacturer. Even though equipment manufacturers had rejected me previously – that remained my goal.

Even so, although you've created a great product that is unique to the market and is virtually selling itself, you might assume that the leading manufacturers in that market would welcome you with open arms. But could I get an audience with the big guys? Not a chance...

Throughout my first year in business, I again

reached out to every major print-equipment manufacturer, a few of them two or three times. One door after another slammed in my face. The nearest I got was with MBO America.

I'd developed my first device for an MBO folding machine, several thousand of which were scattered throughout the U.K., including at my place of employment, Streamline Press. So, from the beginning, I'd figured I had a good chance of securing a meeting with the MBO product manager in Germany. That had been my first call the day I'd received my patent-pending notice – and my first rejection.

Six months later, I again tried the product manager at MBO Germany, but he wouldn't even take my calls. So I contacted the head of the MBO dealership in the U.K., hoping he'd introduce me to the main guy in Germany. He told me straight out that, even if my device could do what I claimed it did, MBO wasn't interested because they had their own solution to the cracking problem, the Super-Score, which their customers and technical staff were perfectly happy with.

This was so frustrating to me because I knew some of his sales reps as well as he did, and they were telling me a different story. I knew the Super-Score inside and out because I'd tried it many times myself, never with good results. I'd also seen many Super-Scores being taken off folding machines up and down the U.K. to make way for my Tri-Creaser.

Undeterred, I turned my attention to MBO America. Through my research I'd found out that the U.S. division of MBO had the ability to purchase ancillary equipment without running it past the German headquarters. I dreamed of making it big in America, who didn't – and knew that the U.S. market was about eight times bigger than the U.K.'s. I exchanged a few emails with the vice president of MBO America, who expressed interest in the Tri-Creaser but still referred me to his main technician, the person who would say yes or no.

Then I made a crucial mistake: Rather than scheduling a demo at MBO, as I'd expected, I agreed to send my device to the technician for testing, without me being there. The guy assured me he was an expert, citing his 30 years of experience in training folding-machine operators.

What I didn't know until after I'd shipped the device was that the technician was the very person who had developed the Super-Score. That the gatekeeper to my future with MBO was testing my device against a competitive product that he'd developed did not bode well. However, I had no choice but to wait for his call.

Within two weeks I received a package in the post with my returned devices, a few weakly scored sheets, and a brief rejection note. The rough creases looked alien to me – totally unlike the tens of thousands of smooth creases produced by my Tri-Creaser to date. I was fuming – which led straight to my next mistake: I called this guy and let my frustration be known. I suggested that the samples weren't produced using my device and that he either set it wrong or doctored the results. I was on the verge of losing my temper, but thankfully, had the sense to rein it all in.

The technician (who, incidentally, was British) claimed that both the processes for printing and producing paper were different in the U.S. from those in the U.K. Therefore, he asserted, my Tri-Creaser would never solve the cracking problem there. Adding salt to my wounds, he boasted that the Super-Score had come out on top in every test he'd conducted. I calmly ended the conversation by stating he may have won the battle but not the war, adding that one day he would have to explain his decision to his superiors.

The Tri-Creaser went on to soundly corner the U.S. creasing market. Over the years, I have been approached many times by MBO America sales and technical personnel wanting to know why they aren't selling Tri-Creasers and have to buy them from an independent distributor. I simply say, "You had the first chance." I've often wondered whether the gatekeeper who blocked my way into MBO America was ever held accountable for that missed opportunity.

When I think back to that incident, I am grateful that it played out as it did. I learned a lot about how to approach global organisations and how to deal with rejection. It also taught me never to send my products out for evaluation without me physically being there.

After the fiasco with MBO America, I targeted another manufacturer called Baumfolder, which had a large share of the folding-machine market in the United States. The person responsible for taking on new products already knew of the Tri-Creaser, and I called him directly. He enthusiastically told me that his company could sell thousands of my products and that he loved the idea of partnering with me. Another phone call later that week got me even more amped up. This guy was on fire for my Tri-Creaser. I thought I'd struck gold, teaming up with someone who was as excited as I was about getting the Tri-Creaser out there in the U.S.

But then the trail went cold.

When I followed up by email to schedule a product demonstration two weeks later, he replied that he didn't need to see the Tri-Creaser. He made no mention of pursuing the matter further, and my dreams of making it big in the States were shattered. He'd built me up... then dropped me like a ton of bricks.

Meanwhile, I'd made a second attempt to arrange a product demonstration at Heidelberg – this time mentioning some of the major companies I had sold to in the U.K. Again, the answer was a firm *no*.

Many of the large manufacturing companies that I have tried to do business with employ people whose responsibilities include evaluating products that have been independently developed to determine whether they're interested in acquiring licensing or manufacturing rights to them. The problem is that many of these gatekeepers end up thwarting, rather than fostering, innovation. Some feel threatened by any idea that might outshine theirs and so reject them. Others are quick to say no to anything they deem "too good to be true," often without the benefit of an objective evaluation. What's more, these gatekeepers often have the authority to make that reject-or-proceed call, with little or no discourse with their peers or superiors.

Dealing with those types of obstructionists and naysayers can either demoralize or motivate you. I've had my fair share of people who have tried to stop or restrict my progress. Some have blocked my way into a company, and some have insulted me to my face. Being dismissed and disrespected never feels good, and I admit that such situations have hurt, frustrated, and angered me. But I've learned that holding on to anger and disappointment only holds you back. I've heard people go on and on about how they got stung in business and now they don't trust anyone, and view business as nasty or dark, and are always on the defensive. I don't see any point in being in business if it makes you go around with a bitter attitude, suspicious of everyone.

In fact, I've found that being treated poorly or unfairly also has a positive side. It spurs me to improve my performance and sharpen my focus. Having a bit of a chip on your shoulder can be good – as long as it's the kind that motivates you to do better and *not* the kind that makes you resentful.

Passion And Persistence Pay Off

As my first year in business drew to an end, I eventually sold a few Tri-Creasers to a folding-machine dealership in the United Kingdom. To clinch the sale, I'd modified my device to fit a folding machine manufactured by a German company called Mathias Bauerle. To show their appreciation, the dealership told the manufacturer about what I'd done, which prompted Mathias Bauerle to order 20 Tri-Creasers and invite me to visit them in Germany. Progress.

Of course, Heidelberg – the world's largest and my top choice of equipment manufacturers to team up with – is also based in Germany. So I tried one more time to fix up a meeting while I was in the country anyway. The product manager seemed agitated and surprised that I had called him yet again to request a meeting. Despite his insistence that "it wouldn't be worth my plane fare," he agreed, reluctantly, to see me – more, I suspect, out of wanting to put an end to my pursuit in person, than to actually see my Tri-Creaser. Finally after more than twelve months and several rejections, I had a demo with Heidelberg

In preparation for the meeting, I reviewed the information I'd previously gathered on Heidelberg and did additional research on the company. I knew the types of folding machines they produced as well as the devices and solutions they used for scoring. Indeed, I'd utilized those tools and processes myself. For the more difficult substrates, Heidelberg had created a tool similar to MBO's Super-Score –basically, a metal disc harnessed in a collar that ran into a bed of rubber. That device was among the collection of orphaned scoring attachments I had tried and were gathering dust on the shelves on the back wall at Streamline Press. It just didn't do the job.

My meeting with Heidelberg preceded the one at Mathias Bauerle. With another folding-machine manufacturer hugely interested in stocking a version of my product and with over 200 devices sold, I felt cautiously optimistic. Even though I was keenly aware that a deal with Heidelberg could push my Tri-Creaser worldwide, I wasn't desperate. Regardless of what happened that day, I had a good business with an exciting future.

My game plan was the same as the one I'd successfully employed numerous times with printing companies. I'd listen respectfully to the product manager, and play it cool. Rather than showing a brochure or sell sheet and talking up my innovation, as experts often advise and many inventors do, I'd let the demonstration do the talking for me. Then, in the afterglow of the decision-maker having witnessed first-hand the flawless creases produced by the Tri-Creaser, I would discuss features, benefits, and pricing. Only later did I learn that big manufacturers usually allow only a few minutes and dictate the procedure for such meetings. That said, I still believe in my way and have always found it to be successful in these types of face-to-face meetings.

Upon my arrival at Heidelberg's impressive Post

Press headquarters in Ludwigsburg, the product manager that met me seemed polite enough – at least until he asked to see the Tri-Creaser. As I opened the box, he glanced inside and curtly declared, "That is similar to ours and a possible infringement."

I calmly pointed out the O-ring and other unique features that clearly distinguished the Tri-Creaser from Heidelberg's scoring device. Then, I politely explained that during my research I'd noticed that their scoring attachment wasn't patented. Admittedly, in hindsight, that was a rather risky statement, as I was effectively telling him that even if my device *was* similar to Heidelberg's, I couldn't be guilty of infringement

The product manager looked shocked by my comment, but quickly gathered himself and moved on to his next question. But I couldn't help noticing that – from that point forward – he seemed to think more carefully before speaking.

We finished our coffee, and I expressed how impressed I was with the facility in Ludwigsburg and asked if I could have a look around. The product manager seemed to mellow as he proudly gave me a mini-tour of the showroom. Once we returned to the meeting area, however, his mood reverted to its former curtness. He announced that I had one hour to prove that my product was a significant improvement to Heidelberg's solution. While the two of us went to lunch, he went on, his technicians would use the Tri-Creaser to run through a black cover stock that had been giving them grief. If my device stopped the cracking problem, then we would talk.

Although – after the MBO America debacle – I'd vowed never again to allow my product to be tested without me being present, this time I felt the odds were in my favour. I knew without a shadow of a doubt that my device would perform circles around Heidelberg's device and that printing companies would continue to buy the Tri-Creaser, whether directly from me or from a reseller. Heidelberg had more to lose by not giving it a fair shot than I did. Plus, at least I was in the building, not on the other side of the world.

I spent about ten minutes instructing the technicians how to fit the Tri-Creaser to the folding machine in their showroom. Then, off the product manager and I went to a café, leaving my future with Heidelberg in the hands of the technicians. Although I had every confidence my Tri-Creaser would blow their scoring device out of the water, I could only trust my device would get a more fair trial than I'd received at MBO America.

After lunch, as the product manager and I approached the showroom, one of the technicians rushed out to meet us in the corridor. In one hand he held sheets with badly cracked spines. In the other he held sheets with perfectly smooth creases – exactly like those produced previously by my device. It was a defining moment, and I felt so proud and elated, but I kept it inside.

The product manager asked the technician which batch had been scored using the Tri-Creaser. My heart skipped a beat, and for a fleeting second I thought, *What if he doesn't point at the good copies? What if my dream is about to end?*

I need not have worried. His finger rested squarely on the un-cracked spines, and with that my heart soared.

The product manager and technician had a brief discussion in German, and I guessed the product manager was trying to extract details about what had just happened. Once again, the Tri-Creaser had taken centre stage and I was insignificant in comparison. But this wasn't a demonstration where I could stand by ready to collect a cheque. I had to stay composed and stick to the rest of my plan.

The product manager looked surprised and angry about the outcome, and I was perplexed why he would act that way. He rather forcibly demanded that we go to his office for further discussion, after which he sat me at his meeting table while he called in a few colleagues. Three gentlemen in sharp suits joined the product manager on the other side of the table. One gentleman, the global purchasing manager, spoke softly. The other two executives were quite abrupt. They spoke briefly among themselves in German and exchanged slight nods.

Suddenly, the product manager thumped his fist on the table and suggested I cancel any further dealings with Mathias Bauerle and agree not to sell to anyone else because Heidelberg wanted to manufacture my product, subject to further testing.

I allowed the suggestion to hang in the air for a moment. I'd known going in what the Tri-Creaser meant to so many of my customers and therefore what it *could* mean for Heidelberg. Now, these guys wanted to prise the star performer out of my grasp – and it was time for me to rise up to the mark. I'd come ready for the task, and I delivered my response with measured consideration.

First, I told them that if they would have seen me a year earlier, when I'd first offered a demonstration, they might have got that kind of deal. However, during that year I'd sold 200 units with ease and proved how unique and in demand my solution was. The product manager didn't look at all impressed, but I didn't care. I was playing hardball now – albeit without their scowls and acerbic tones.

Then, I calmly but emphatically stated that I would not cancel any dealings or appointments with other manufacturers with an interest in doing business with me.

One of the more aggressive negotiators suggested I allow Heidelberg to manufacture the Tri-Creaser and they'd pay me royalties. I told them I was not interested in that sort of deal. Another speculated that they would get zero sales if their customers knew the device was made in England. I assured them there would be no problem with the quality of my product, for which I intended to retain manufacturing rights and to offer them a good discounted price as a reseller.

My research had told me that any licensing deals would have brought me 5–7 per cent of the sale price of each unit. The Tri-Creaser was never going to be a product that Heidelberg would sell tens of thousands of per year. In fact, earlier in the meeting one of the three negotiators had revealed they'd sold only 200 of their rubber-bed scoring devices globally. Even if we doubled that with Heidelberg making the product, I knew from my earlier calculations that a licensing deal would bring me a maximum of £10,000 per year in royalties. That did not represent good business.

In contrast, if Heidelberg *purchased* my device at 30 per cent off the retail price and sold, say, 400 units, my return would be close to £100,000. Granted, with Heidelberg manufacturing my Tri-Creaser, they would have had more incentive to sell 1,000 units per year, maybe even 2,000. However, such numbers could potentially harm my chances of setting up distribution outlets, due to the competition, and my returns would probably equate to little more than what I'd earned at my day job per year, although admittedly I wouldn't need to do anything to earn it.

Another of the negotiators argued that Heidelberg was better equipped to develop the full Tri-Creaser product range because they have a department and several technicians dedicated to research and development. Each of the negotiators, in their way, insinuated that I'd gotten lucky with this one and they would take over now. *Was this tongue in cheek?* I wondered, or *just the type of tactics big companies employ to try to unsettle people like me, who bring good products to their door?* Either way, it didn't work. I did not succumb to such heavy-handed tactics, nor did I allow myself to feel pressured.

Smiling confidently, I told them I was no one-trick pony. I declined every suggestion of this nature and actually enjoyed the experience. I sensed we would end up doing business, but I knew I needed to hold firm to make sure that I dictated the narrative and secured the best terms.

However, after we discussed the possibility of my company supplying the Tri-Creaser to Heidelberg at a 30 per cent discount, I was given an ultimatum: Allow Heidelberg to manufacture the Tri-Creaser and pay me royalties, or walk away.

I walked away.

Exactly one week to the day later, Heidelberg's global purchasing manager called to place an order for 500 Tri-Creasers and to set up a one-year purchasing contract. I was ecstatic. We had yet to negotiate the pricing and I had to agree to let them rename the device Channel Score, but I was delighted with the outcome regardless. Although I agreed to a slightly bigger discount, since it was such a major order, the Heidelberg deal set me on my way to global distribution of the Tri-Creaser and pulled in around £100,000 in profits in little more than a year.

> *"Many of life's failures are people who did not realize how close they were to success when they gave up."* — Thomas Edison

Hindsight Really Is 20/20

When I first reached out to Heidelberg and other folding-machine manufacturers, within days of receiving my patent-pending notification, I felt vulnerable – like my idea was too big for me. At that point, selling my device outright, handing over my patents to an industry leader that actually knew what to do with it, seemed like my best and perhaps only option. I had no understanding of how much money that might bring me. Since Fireman Mick's friend had been offered £500,000 for his life-saving invention, I speculated that maybe I could sell my invention for, say, £100,000. (Instead, I'd made that amount in clear profit with my first Heidelberg order alone).

In reality, as I would later learn, my odds of selling a first-of-its-kind, unproven idea with no sales and no performance track record, which purportedly did what no one in the print industry believed could be done, was slim to none – for *any* price, much less six figures. Even if some company had given me a chance to show them my invention and had been interested in acquiring or licensing my idea, I had only patent-pending status at the time. So the value of my device then was minimal, and the possibility of the patent not being granted posed a significant risk to the manufacturer.

In retrospect, those product managers were just doing their job diligently. I probably didn't help my case, either. I was very inexperienced, with zero knowledge about how to present a new product – far less pitching an industry-changing new technology to a large corporation. At the time, in 1999, there were no TV reality shows like *Dragon's Den* and *Shark Tank* and few online resources for independent inventors. I also had the rather casual attitude that I could make my mark in the world and change my life with the least amount of effort.

Today, I can see both sides of the situation. I understand the inventor who feels 10 feet tall for having created a great product and thinks he or she'll hit the jackpot by calling some important contact and proclaiming the wonders of his or her idea. I can also understand the irritation of the manufacturer's gatekeeper who has to constantly field queries from persistent inventors claiming to have developed the next best thing. Given how tenaciously I tried to get my foot in the door, I must have been especially irritating.

I've sometimes wondered what might have happened had one of those gatekeepers agreed to a product demo while I was still relatively clueless. I might well have sold my idea outright for £2,000 or given up manufacturing rights for a 7 per cent royalty. Then, I wouldn't have made a £60,000 profit selling 200 devices on my own that first year. Nor would I have started off the second year by selling 500 devices to the world's largest print-equipment manufacturer for resale to their customers. Nor would I be writing this book about how a print finisher created a thriving, growing £20 million global brand.

Being turned down by the big guys, even for a product demonstration, was the best thing that could have happened to me at that early stage of the game. Had I managed to get an audience, I most likely would have been eaten alive. Not only did I have no sales and no testimonials from satisfied customers, I also had no pricing structure and no marketing literature. I hadn't even named my product!

Those early dismissals by industry leaders forced me to get out there and prove the value of my product by selling it and building a cache of happy customers myself. Those twelve months of hands-on experience taught me so much about my product, my customers, and myself. It enabled me to polish my presentation and improve my business skills. It boosted my confidence and empowered me to create a vision for my *own* company.

The more rejections I received and the more direct sales I acquired that first year, the stronger my conviction became that I should retain manufacturing rights and keep control of marketing and distributing the Tri-Creaser. What I'd failed to realize at the starting gate, when I started taking my idea to the next level seemed beyond my capabilities, was that I, Graham Harris, was the perfect person to bring my product to market. With my experience and knowledge of the problem I'd set out to solve and the available solutions for it, I knew the market potential of my technology better than the manufacturers I was trying to convince to take it on. That is why their rejections didn't destroy my belief.

One person with an idea born out of passion, knowledge, and the will to succeed can often surpass the global corporations with their marketing experts and R&D staff, who typically have less desire and incentive to innovate. Some of the greatest ideas come from individuals who are driven by the dream to change the world and their own lives.

Chapter 4

Shout It from the Rooftops!

A BIG MOTIVATOR behind the decision to take my invention to market myself was that nobody else believed the claims I was making about my new technology. Remember, initially, no investors or marketers were begging me to let them come on board, and no resellers or licensors were letting me in when I came knocking. That left me no option but to sell my device directly to end users – printing and print-finishing companies. It was the only way to prove my product in the marketplace and to satisfy myself that I could make a business out of my idea.

And time was of the essence...

I'd given myself one year to sell 100 Tri-Creasers. I needed those proceeds to cover patent fees, pay back the loan from my sister, and develop additional versions of my product. Also, there was a twelve-month waiting period from the date I'd filed for my U.K. patent before I could file for international patents. Therefore, to justify the considerable expense of patenting and marketing worldwide, I needed to first secure enough successful installations to substantiate that there was, indeed, a global market for my product.

By the end of that first year, I'd sold over 200 devices. I'd also secured a reseller deal and an initial purchase order for 500 Tri-Creasers from Heidelberg – the print industry's largest original equipment manufacturer (OEM) and equipment reseller.

How, you might ask, did I – a print finisher with no background in marketing, no time to get schooled in marketing, and no means to hire a marketing agency

– manage to successfully launch a new technology in a mature market in which innovations were few and far between?

Frankly, by the seat of my pants – set on fire by the same passion for creative problem-solving and by the same fear of failure that had led me to invent my rotary creaser in the first place. Following my instincts, I improvised and learned as I went, and there was much more to learn about marketing than I'd ever imagined.

On A Wing And A Prayer

When I decided to bring my product to market myself, I had no clue where to start. I was truly flying blind – propelled as much by desperation as by my conviction that the Tri-Creaser was the answer to every print finisher's prayers, if only they would give it a chance.

Despite my lack of marketing know-how, logic told me I needed some kind of handout for potential customers. After all, my device was unlike anything on the market, and it did something no one believed could be done. As soon as I received my patent-pending notice, my wife, Sue, and I put together a marketing leaflet featuring a black-and-white snapshot of the Tri-Creaser, a product description, and contact information. In describing the Tri-Creaser, I tried to put myself in the customers' shoes, citing the product features they'd want to know and the benefits it offered them. Of course, the Tri-Creaser's main attribute – that it eliminated cracking on the fold – was stated front and centre.

Even though I'd developed my device to be simple to install and use, the settings applied on customers' sites also had to be precise in order for the Tri-Creaser to work its magic. So I also created a users' guide for customers in the absence of me standing beside them showing them how to do it. This one-page document consisted of step-by-step written instructions and corresponding images showing exactly how to achieve each setting.

Both the marketing leaflet and users' guides were generated in Microsoft Word by a friend who owned a computer and desktop printer – two items that Sue and I didn't even own at the time. We sent photocopies of the leaflet to prospects and gave photocopies of the users' guide to customers with their newly purchased Tri-Creasers.

From the beginning, I'd also realised that I couldn't just carry the Tri-Creasers in my hand or a briefcase when demonstrating or delivering my product to customers. To give at least a semblance of professionalism, I needed some kind of packaging. Initially, that consisted of a plain, white cardboard box, which I purchased from a local vendor in three sizes. The components of each Tri-Creaser were encased in bubble wrap and fitted snugly into the respective box for that model.

Those first attempts at "marketing materials" were basic and no doubt came across as rather makeshift. In retrospect, they certainly didn't do justice to the world-class product for which they were created. But we did the best we could with what we had, and it was enough to get me started. I was so intent on getting word out about my ground-breaking new device that I refused to let my lack of marketing expertise hold me back. Really I was oblivious to how little I knew about what I was trying to do.

Therein lies one advantage to being naïve: You don't know what you don't know. But, if your naivety happens to be accompanied by determination and an adventurous spirit, as mine was, you can do things you never imagined you could – including marketing. Your methods may be unconventional and the results less than ideal, but doing your best beats doing nothing at all, especially when it comes to getting a new product in front of potential customers. Then, after you've gained the knowledge and resources to do better, you can and *should* up your game, which is precisely what I did.

Later that first year, with more experience under my belt and a bit more cash in hand, I revamped the marketing leaflet with the help of a friend who had some graphic design experience. Fortunately, that co-incided with the launch of our mail-order program, which also prompted me to improve the users' guide to make it even easier for customers to install the Tri-Creaser without me being there.

We also upgraded the product packaging. I con-tracted with a local company to produce a custom-made foam sleeve with two holes to brace the steel device and a pouch to hold the creasing O-rings – as well as a custom-made double-fluted box into which the foam sleeve was inserted. Attractive and sturdy, the packag-ing stood up to the rigors of shipping, handsomely dis-played the device when the box was opened, and gave customers a safe place to house their Tri-Creasers. The professional packaging made my product stand out and added value, and was well worth the £5 per unit cost.

After securing plentiful sales throughout that first year and starting the second year in a similar fashion, I became concerned when sales dipped slightly in early spring of the next. I wanted to build momentum, not lose it, and my research told me I'd only scratched the surface of the U.K. market for my product. In fact, I had grabbed the low-hanging fruit – sales that had been relatively easy to procure.

Research suggests that a small segment of any market is always quick to buy the latest thing – particularly when it's a first of its kind product and sounds too good to be true, like my Tri-Creaser. And when those kinds of people catch wind of a new and exciting product or service, they can often be persuaded to hop on board with moderate effort on your part. And thank heavens for those believers. Without knowing it, they gave me the sales experience and confidence I needed to get a foothold in the market during that wild first year of essentially hawking my product door to door. Furthermore, and very significantly for us as a family, the profits from those "easy" sales had also enabled me to quit my gloomy day job and forge an exciting new career for myself.

However, after a year of skimming the cream off the top, I began to run into what looked like scepticism in the market. Meeting with that wall of resistance only prompted me to do even more to promote my Tri-Creaser. First, I put together an advertisement and placed it in *Printweek* magazine. Unfortunately, the advert bombed. I didn't understand why, and I was hesitant to spend more money on advertising when the first advert had failed to generate a single lead. So I decided to focus on getting more free publicity.

"Don't be intimidated by what you don't know. That can be your greatest strength and ensure that you do things differently from everyone else." — Sara Blakely

Unleashing The Power Of Free Publicity

Public relations are the art and science of enlisting the media to communicate positive stories about a person, product, or business – free of charge. Of course, publicists and PR firms charge plenty to secure editorial coverage on behalf of their clients. Few lone inventors and early-stage entrepreneurs can afford to hire such experts, and many avoid seeking publicity on their own under the mistaken notion that it's out of their league. Nothing could be further from the truth.

My first foray into public relations via the article in *Printweek*, had been a revelation. And it had been easier to obtain and more effective than I'd expected.

I'd simply called the editor and told her I'd invented a device that eliminated a major problem for printers and that my first customer was eager to share how my product had helped his company. After I agreed to give *Printweek* exclusive rights to my "breaking" story, the editor handed me over to a reporter, Gordon Carson. During our interview, Gordon expressed enthusiasm about writing the article, saying it was a "refreshing change" from the usual news about the merger or liquidation of a big corporation. He also interviewed my customer, Vic Furness, the print manager at Polestar in Bradford.

I was so pleased with Gordon's article – not least because it was easy to spot, at the top of page five and with a bold headline announcing, "Innovative solution to printers' creasing hassles." Although the piece was short, it included the key benefit of my device, a complimentary quote from Vic Furness, and my telephone number. At that early stage, that was all that was required.

We were flooded with calls from printing shops throughout the U.K., requesting product demonstrations, the majority of which resulted in sales. Just like that, my product was launched, and I'd spent next to nothing on marketing.

So, several months later – after I'd exhausted the leads generated by the *Printweek* article, and sales took a slight dip, and then seeing my advert fail – I decided to drum up some more free publicity. I started by contacting our local newspaper, the *Leicester Mercury*, and inviting them to share my story. I strategically played the "poor lone inventor" card again, even going so far as to state I was surprised that no printing-equipment manufacturers were knocking on my door asking to market my ground-breaking device themselves.

The article, which appeared in the Business News section of the newspaper, lauded the success of a local "clever inventor" who had "succeeded through a high degree of scepticism" and "without financial help from bankers, investors, or business partners." The editorial generated considerable interest from local printing companies, many of which became customers.

Protect Your Public Image

Some journalists and publishers like to "spin" a story to make it "more sensational". If that spin sends the wrong message about you, your product, or your business, the publicity can do more harm than good. I found myself in that uncomfortable position when the reporter assigned to write the local-inventor-makes-good article in our local newspaper wanted a photo of me throwing £50 notes in the air. I refused, politely explaining that it was against both my business ethics and my Christian beliefs. The article ended up being smaller than we'd originally spoken about, but I preferred that to projecting an image that was contrary to my values and might offend customers. If you don't like the way a reporter or producer plans to depict you or your brand, raise your objections and refuse permission to run the story with the objectionable content.

Over the next few years, I fed stories to the media on a regular basis. At the time, I reached out primarily to trade magazines and local newspapers. These days, your options may also include radio, television, blogs, podcasts, social media, and other online media.

Securing publicity came naturally to me. I studied the contents of each publication and got to know the various editors and journalists. I'd come up with different story angles that fitted the publications' editorial scopes – so that the content might be of interest to its readers.

Sometimes I'd focus on the quick return of investment that the Tri-Creaser offered customers. Other times, I'd focus on the quality-improvement or timesaving aspect of my product. I often included a testimonial quote from a customer too. Along with my cover letter and press release, I usually added a one-page document that summarised the main talking points of the story I was proposing. Sometimes, I would spend all day producing a press packet, testing which story line worked best, sourcing facts, and adding images.

Every time we got media coverage, leads rolled in and sales went up. But I knew I couldn't rely solely on free publicity forever. At some point, those editors and reporters would need to pass me on to their advertising department, and the ad reps would want to see the colour of my money. Given the failure of my first advert, however, I was reluctant to jump back into the advertising arena without first getting some professional coaching. As fate would have it, the article in the *Leicester Mercury* had attracted the attention of a marketing guru.

Bringing In A Pro

About a week after the *Leicester Mercury* article was published, I received a letter from Steve Hackney, a local marketing consultant and former rugby star for the Leicester Tigers. Steve's letter was personal and polite, congratulating me on my progress and spelling out how he could help me realize the potential of my product. He included a list of the companies he had supported as well as testimonials from clients that spoke of him helping to triple or quadruple their profits. The letter ended with the offer of a full refund if his efforts failed to at least double our current sales within three months. Sue and I discussed this in great detail and our immediate thought was: *What's the catch? Is this too good to be true?*

Then I remembered that was exactly what some of my potential customers thought about my invention. So we decided to at least meet with Steve to hear what he had to say. I called and invited him to our home, where we'd turned a front room into an office and the kitchen doubled as an assembly and packaging centre.

Steve understood our situation, and we got on well straight away. From the outset Steve told me that if we were to work together, he needed my trust. He knew I'd have doubts about some of his "unconventional" marketing strategies and he wanted some license to carry them out. He explained we would need to overhaul what we'd been doing and that he would have to systematize our operation, not that we had much of one anyway.

At that point, I showed Steve the advert I had created. He could have sneered or laughed at it and told me everything that was wrong with it. Instead, he restated with calm authority that he was confident his strategies would substantially increase our leads, sales, and profits. He then reiterated his offer to refund all the money he would charge for the first three months of our collaboration if we didn't hit the numbers.

Then it came down to Steve's charge to develop a marketing and sales program over a two-month period, during which he would provide a progress report twice a month, and to help me implement the program in the third month. His fee was as much as I would have been paid for a month of 50-hour workweeks in my previous place of employment! Sue and I both liked Steve and were impressed with his credentials and professionalism, but we were sceptical. After talking it over briefly, though, we decided to take him up on his offer, figuring we could recover the fee if it didn't work out and the rewards would be great if it did.

For two months Steve did little more than learn about my company and my product, unearthing several benefits I hadn't thought of. He also set up a lead-generation process that utilized a customer relationship management (CRM) software package for storing contact information, logging interactions with prospects and customers, tracking sales, and measuring results.

Next, Steve created an advert and a series of letters to send to people who responded to the ad. He explained the importance of not trying to sell our Tri-Creaser straight off the advert and of using the letters to address the prospects' hesitance and build their confidence in my product.

For the advert and letters, I provided him with customer testimonials and input about the functionality of the Tri-Creaser. He liked my Tri-Creaser brochure but requested that I add more benefits and features. That's when I showed Steve a photo I'd recently had taken of two bunches of leaflets, one stack showing cracking on the folds caused by a scoring device and the other with flawless folds that had been creased with the Tri-Creaser. His eyes lit up! He placed that photo at the top and centre of the advert, because, he said, it would draw in potential customers and they could see the results with their own eyes.

When Steve showed me the finished ad and the first letter he intended us to send, I was almost paralyzed with shock. I didn't like the style at all – which seemed to be exactly what my contacts at the advertising departments of the printing magazines had warned me against: wordy and cheap-looking. It looked like a three-column article with a bold headline. Adding to the tabloid-like look of the ad was a fill-in-the-blank form for requesting additional information that people were to cut out and mail in.

To make matters worse, Steve asked me to spend £1,000 to place the *full-page* advert on an early right-hand page of *Printweek*!

I told Steve that the advert didn't convey the image I wanted for my company, that no one would read all those words, and that we needed to start over with a more corporate look and less copy.

He stared squarely into my eyes and asked me an important question that applies to anyone considering placing an advert for anything: "Do you want big sales or a pretty advert that gets a few leads but no sales?"

I cringed inwardly, remembering and wondering whether Steve was hinting at my handsome ad that had failed miserably.

(In the years to come, Steve Hackney and a few other consultants in his company would use my advert as an example of how *not* to advertise. Apparently, it broke all the rules: It had a weak headline. It cited hardly any benefits. It featured an image of a shiny Tri-Creaser, a device no one knew about, sitting on a table doing nothing. And it had no call to action).

Steve then reminded me that I had given him my trust to do what he thought would work – based, I might add, on his well-demonstrated expertise.

With a degree of trepidation, I agreed to move forward with his campaign.

The ad appeared in the next issue of *Printweek*. The response blew me away. Day after day, our mail-box filled with those tawdry vouchers. In total, we got 65 requests for information.

Each information packet included a sales letter, customer testimonials, and an order form. If we didn't receive an order from someone who had responded to the ad within a predetermined period of time, we sent the second letter with another order form. We sent the third letter and an order form to those who didn't re-spond to either the first or second letters. Almost 40 of those prospects purchased Tri-Creasers, and most of them bought two or three devices each. From that one ad, we made about £25,000 profit.

We repeated Steve's direct-response campaign several times, with similar results. What's more, many of the prospects who didn't buy straight away became customers later on. Sue and I often look back on this period as the most exciting time in our business journey. By then we had employed my friend and former colleague, Paul Barrett to look after the sales, and Sue's friend, Wendy Austen, who took care of sending out the information packs, building the database, packing devices and despatching them all over the U.K. Sue virtually ran the business side of things, dealing with the finances, office operation and mail order systemization, leaving Steve and me to generate and implement marketing strategies to get my products into the market.

Steve then created a powerful website for Techni-Fold that included an e-commerce section, in part to help attract and handle international sales. We sold hundreds of Tri-Creasers into the U.S.A. and also did well in Australia, New Zealand and some other English speaking regions. Every morning, I'd sign into our site and see all the orders and the money going into our bank account. It was so exciting.

Set The Optimal Price For Your Product

One of the most important decisions you'll make is what to charge for your product. Charge too much, and your product won't sell well. Charge too little, and it cuts into profits and can position your product at a low level in the market. The longer a product is sold at a price that is either too low or too high, the more difficult it is to increase or decrease the price without adverse repercussions from the market.

One of the first things Steve Hackney did after I hired him was to calculate that, on average, our customers were getting a return on their investment in the Tri-Creaser within three job runs. Before we ran the first advert Steve had created for us, he convinced Sue and me to increase our selling price from £395 to £499. Luckily, neither our returning nor our new customers objected to the higher price. Later, Steve did additional price testing that enabled us to go up to £599 and then £699 after adding a couple of simple features to the product.

Steve Hackney advocated "marketing within your means," contending that "big-brand agency marketing" and conventional sales strategies were inappropriate for most small and medium-size businesses. He put together an affordable and effective marketing program that more than substantially drove up our sales. Furthermore, his strategies reduced the time and cost of generating leads and making sales, which increased our profits.

Steve and I worked well together, brainstorming creative ways to generate leads and increase sales, and he knew how to execute every idea we came up with. As time went on, his guidance helped us to improve every aspect of our sales and marketing – from our adverts to our direct-response packets, logo, product packaging, and trade-show exhibits.

Our company was profitable and growing when Steve came onto the scene, but he gave us that shot in the arm that fast-tracked our success. Steve Hackney inspired me, taught me, and helped me take my business to the next level.

Learning The Tricks Of The Trade Show

Most independent inventors and early-stage entrepreneurs fantasise about showcasing and selling their new creations at a trade show – understandably. Exhibiting at a trade show can be a highly effective marketing strategy. But exhibiting a new product too soon – before you've mastered your sales pitch, refined your product packaging and promo materials, sold enough product to prove its commercial viability, and learned how to effectively utilize trade shows – is one of the most common and costly mistakes made by independent inventors and early-stage entrepreneurs. When you exhibit at a trade expo, you are judged by the same criteria as all other exhibitors. If you come across as a greenhorn, you will be treated like one – that is, not seriously.

Like most people who create products, I was gung-ho to market my ground-breaking creasing device at trade expos. Fortunately, I didn't have the money to exhibit at a trade show until after I'd sold a bunch of Tri-Creasers and hired Steve Hackney to help step up my marketing game. Prior to that, however, I did manage to attend my first trade show, where I also managed to annoy my first major reseller, Heidelberg.

A few months into my second year of business, I went to the world's largest print trade show, Drupa, in Germany to see my Tri-Creaser on display in Heidelberg's booth and to look for business contacts. I went independently and at my own expense, without invitation from and without informing the product manager at Heidelberg. I was so excited! I was also well prepared, having researched the exhibitors, mapped out which booths I'd check out, and brought along leaflets to hand out at the show. I made dozens of valuable contacts and sold a lot of Tri-Creasers, but I might have pushed too far. The Heidelberg product manager caught on to me and was not pleased. I had to dodge him as I made my rounds, pitching my product and distributing my leaflets. But I just had to grab that opportunity with both hands.

The following year, our company exhibited for the first time at another major print-industry trade show. Although we had one of the smaller spaces in a less-trafficked area, we came up with a way to grab people's attention and draw them into our booth for a live product demonstration. Steve Hackney had created an interactive novelty leaflet and instructed us to stand at the perimeter of our booth and hand out the leaflet to passers-by. I felt uncomfortable with pestering people as they strolled by, but Steve literally insisted. Our tactic did turn some people away, but Steve had been right. Nonchalantly passing out those quirky leaflets brought a lot of foot traffic into our stand, much more than to neighbouring booths. Once people entered our stand and saw the Tri-Creaser do its magic, many put in their orders, if not during the show then shortly after.

Visit First – Exhibit Later

You can get schooled on the do's and don'ts of trade shows from books, articles, blogs, and other resources produced by marketing experts. But the best way to learn the ropes is to attend at least one trade show as a visitor and careful observer. First, choose a trade show where vendors of products similar to your exhibit. Do visit the booths of competitors and business partners, but then walk the aisles and look at every exhibit with a discerning eye. Study the booths that pull you in as well as those that are busy. What makes them stand out? What is attracting and holding the attention of visitors? Is their display or presentation exceptional in some way? Are they handing out novelty gifts, or holding a draw for a free product or a prize, or giving out free product samples, or offering a discount to showgoers? Then, borrow and adapt whatever might work well for you when the time is right to exhibit at a trade show.

Over the years, we have exhibited at numerous trade shows, using many of Steve Hackney's strategies and some of our own – usually with great results. We choose our venues wisely, and never exhibit simply for the sake of exhibiting. We always have a main purpose in mind for a particular show – whether it is to generate sales leads and sell products, or to introduce a new product or product enhancement, or to seek out business partners. We work out our theme for the show, and we plan out and prepare our strategy for achieving both our main objective and any secondary objectives. We publicise our upcoming participation in the event by posting notices on social media and by sending invitations to visit our booth to customers, prospective customers, and business associates. Often, I also try to secure an article in a trade magazine that is covering the show, pitching a story that somehow ties into the theme of our exhibit and aiming for the issue that appears just before or just after the show.

We always try to come up with a clever way to draw people into our stand, but we've found that it is best to keep it on-point. One time our North American distributor, Technifold U.S.A., hired a magician. Although the magic show did pull in a crowd, the audience stayed only for his performance because it had no relation to our products or business. There is no point in entertaining visitors on your booth if you don't also educate them and/or entice them to look into doing business with you.

Our trade-show presence is customer interactive. The Tech-ni-Fold booth is usually constructed in an educational format so that visitors can learn how and why our solutions work and also see them in action. I like to keep our pitch short and simple, leading with the unique selling proposition (U.S.P) for that product (which now includes several other devices in addition to the Tri-Creaser). For instance, we've often featured the tag line: *The Tri-Creaser will completely eliminate fibre-cracking on your folding machine or your money back* on a large banner above the photograph of brochures with smooth folds next to brochures with cracked folds. Every time we've used that type of banner or display, we've had people queuing up in the aisles.

> *"People will make leaps of faith and get excited about your product if you just get in front of them."* — James Dyson

Marketing A Growing, Global Brand

When I first hired Steve Hackney, he told me I would need him for only twelve to eighteen months, at which point I'd be set up to carry his strategies forward on my own. Steve was with us for almost five years when I decided the time had come to part ways. We weren't generating as many leads or sales at the ratio we had become accustomed to – and some of Steve's ideas weren't sparking quite the same interest in the market-place. Steve's consultancy was growing and his fee was rising. My business had also matured, and I wanted to build the brand a little differently, using most of the marketing techniques Steve had taught us but also at-tempting some fresh approaches.

As my alliance with Steve seemed as if it was nearing its natural end, I began to look at other business channels for growing the company, especially the international aspect of the business. My conclusion – after considerable research, thought, and discussion with Sue – was that our future was with our distributors. And since distributors process and fill their own customer orders out of their inventory, we removed some of the e-commerce elements on our website.

We continued to use the *direct-response* marketing strategy and CRM system that Steve Hackney had set up for us. Over the years, we've modified those techniques to meet our evolving business and market.

One strategy Steve introduced that continued to be highly effective was our three month money-back guarantee – offering a total refund if our product didn't meet the customer's satisfaction. This was unheard of in the printing industry, and to this day continues to set us apart from competitors and to drive sales.

Free publicity – securing articles and appearances in various media – also continues to be an effective strategy that has been expanded over the years. I wish I'd realized earlier that providing informative content to your target audience is a powerful tool that any business can use to build brand recognition and to promote their products. Some business owners balk at "giving away" information "for free," but I've found that the opposite is true. Creating and publishing blogs, articles, reports, and white papers helps to underpin our expertise and to educate prospects and customers. Ultimately, it has generated qualified leads and sales.

Customer testimonials have always been a key component of our marketing strategy too. Nothing reassures a potential client like resounding endorsement by an existing one. Consequently, we have made a habit of including customer endorsements and case studies in our press releases, editorials, brochures, advertisements, and website. A few years ago, we also started creating customer-testimonial videos and posting them on our website and social media sites, such as YouTube.

Every so often we ask a few of our customers if they would be willing to demonstrate on video how our solutions make a difference in their everyday working environment. We schedule two to three location shoots over a one or two day period, as it is more cost-effective to hire a professional videographer to film multiple videos as one project. I work with the videographer to manage the shoot, and I know in advance what questions we need to ask the customer and what benefits we want our audience to know about. The videos are extremely effective and do a lot of selling for us on our websites.

We've also produced several videos that show customers how to install, maintain, and use our products. These, too, are posted on our website as well as on sites such as YouTube, making them searchable online and easily accessible to both customers and prospective customers. Of course, it also enables us to provide prospects, customers, and business partners with a link to a specific video.

A relatively new marketing piece, introduced in 2013, is actually a customer service tool that is shipped with the product: an installation video card. But it is so attractive and helpful to customers that it adds value to our product and so is marketed as another unique benefit. The free "instant play" video card guides customers step-by-step through the product installation, from unpacking the unit to setting up their first job. It even includes a troubleshooting guide.

I know and work to my strengths and weaknesses, so I don't shoot the videos myself. I hire a professional videographer, and I use a voice-over artist to speak my words on the video. I tested my own untrained voice quite a few times, and it amazed me how the whole message failed. Paying £1,000 for a professional voice-over artist was a good investment, as it has equated to tens of thousands of pounds in profit for a single video.

Another tactic we began after the first *Printweek* article has worked well for us ever since: sending copies of our latest editorial with a Post-it note attached saying something like, "Hi Michael. I thought this might be of interest to you," and signed by one of our staff. The recipient views this as a personal message – even though we've sent the same thing to 5,000 other prospects and customers. This method might seem amateurish to some, and it goes against the corporate-looking typed letter with a sales spiel and call to action advocated by most marketing experts. But there is no denying the results consistently generated by this simple gesture: a marked increase in sales.

Many of our marketing materials still feature a photograph showing a stack of perfectly creased brochures (produced with the Tri-Creaser) next to a stack of brochures with cracked spines (produced with another scoring device). That picture is still worth a thousand words – more than a decade after we first used it in the advert created by Steve Hackney. Our promotional pieces also still highlight the unique value proposition and other benefits of our products. But we've continually expanded and improved our marketing tools over the years. Every brochure, leaflet, product sheet, and other handout is professionally designed and printed, and each has the distinctive look and feel that we've created for our brand.

Likewise, we've continued to improve our packaging. I like our packaging to be slick and colourful – to stand out from the competition and to match the world-class products they contain and protect.

With hindsight, an area of marketing where I could have done better is website development. Our first website, created by Steve Hackney, was great. But then I got so caught up with developing new products and growing the business that I didn't give our site the attention it deserved. Unfortunately, I fell victim to the brigade of web designers who tell you they can market, too, and then don't bother to learn enough about your product, company, or market to do them justice. Once such "web experts" are on board, they have the heart of your business in their hands, and you are shut out of your own website.

One company developed a website for us that worked pretty well, but they charged over the odds for making little tweaks and modifications. I had to buy areas of the website so I could make my own changes. I also paid that company for some online marketing campaigns that didn't work. Every web company I tried ended up being a complete nightmare, so I stopped using them. Our website became stagnant, which no doubt affected sales.

Of course, I learned from those experiences. And it reinforced my belief that the best person to market a brand is the person who created it. We now use Word Press for our website and are not reliant on any third party. It works really well, and we see the Internet as an important component to our growth.

We hired someone to assist me with marketing

strategies, and he is great at online marketing, particularly social media. This channel often leads to great interaction, and we are seeing sales materialise from our social media activities, which include blogging, tweets, LinkedIn posts and adverts, and YouTube.

All of this activity is because I've never been satisfied with the status quo – and my approach to marketing was no exception. If a marketing tactic or tool worked well, I'd use it again and again, tweaking and improving it as I went along, until its effectiveness began to wane. At the same time, I constantly tried to come up with new ways to promote our products and with new incentives to boost sales. It was almost like a game to me, and I enjoyed the challenge.

One year I gave a special holiday discount offer to our customers, and sales went crazy. We struggled to leave the office on Christmas Eve, which didn't please our staff. The two weeks leading up to Christmas are notoriously quiet in the printing industry, and January is usually busy. We had a record-breaking December, but January was our lowest in years. In fact, sales and profits for December and January combined were lower than in the previous six years. My "holiday discount" idea had tanked (Sue did try to warn me). That taught me not to be so hasty in launching a marketing idea – especially when discounting a product that most of our customers are going to buy anyway.

Another spur-of-the-moment idea of mine, however, turned out to be a gift that keeps on giving. One summer, which also tends to be a slow period in the printing industry, I sent out several hundred emails offering customers a free "health check" for their Tech-ni-Fold products and free enhancements to upgrade their existing devices. I think that Lee, our young salesperson, thought I had lost my mind by basically "giving away the goods." He received dozens of emails and phone calls taking up the offer. He then travelled the length and breadth of the U.K. advising customers of how they could get more out of their existing Tech-ni-Fold products with the "free for a limited time" accessories to the devices they already used.

Yes, I wanted to reward our customers for their loyalty. But I also secretly hoped that our gift to them would inspire some of them to buy more products. That wish did not materialize – at least not right away. Then, all of a sudden, we got a rush of paid orders not only for the enhancing accessories but also for our main products. For weeks we were inundated with interest. The moral of the story is that it's amazing how offering something for free can still add to bottom-line profit. Nowadays we repeat this Free Health Check every summer, with the same results.

One of our most successful campaigns featured a video of our manual creasing machine operating next to a traditional method of creasing, clearly demonstrating how our machine matches the quality of the other but outputs six times faster. To the target market, speed is important, and the video plays on their pain of having to use methods that take hours to produce what our machine can produce in minutes. In this video, as with other promo materials, we feature other technology but not an actual brand, because I feel strongly that to do so would be unethical.

Some ideas work and some don't. It isn't always easy science to predict which ones will fly, and which will sink.

"In a crowded marketplace, fitting in is a failure. In a busy marketplace, not standing out is the same as being invisible."
— Seth Godin

It is one of life's tragedies, in my opinion, that so many inventors and entrepreneurs, some 70 to 80 per cent, never realize the wonderful potential of their unique creations because they did not do enough soon enough to let their target market know about their product or business. Once you've progressed through the early patenting stage, you should know the benefits and features of your invention inside and out. You should also know who stands to gain the most from your product.

At that point, you need to do everything within your power to articulate the unique value of your product to your prospective customers. You need to shout it from the rooftops – by whatever means and as frequently as possible.

Even before I applied for a patent, I tracked down all the manufacturers who might want to produce my product, and I contacted every one of them within a week of receiving my patent registration number. When all of those doors slammed shut, I immediately started knocking on the doors of printing companies, offering free demos and a money-back guarantee. Then I started contacting the media and telling my story, soliciting free publicity. When my own marketing efforts did not generate enough leads and sales for my liking, I brought in a marketing expert to help me, and I learned from him as well as from my own mistakes.

Now, my main role is coming up with marketing strategies that work in this day and age. I study marketing trends and spend quite a bit of time researching what other marketers are doing. I meet with our sales and customer service staff regularly, and we brainstorm ways to market our brand. We monitor the results of every marketing strategy we employ. Whatever works well for us we pass on to our distributors. Often, we create a version of one of our successful marketing tactics for them, and sometimes they recreate what we've done using their own resources.

At my core, I am an inventor though.

While I prefer developing products to developing marketing campaigns, I realise how vital marketing is to the success of my business. The only thing I enjoy more than creating products and improving products is seeing my products in use and improving the lives of others. That, after all, was the dream that led me to invent the Tri-Creaser to begin with.

"Anything that won't sell, I don't want to invent. Its sale is proof of utility, and utility is success." — Thomas Edison

Chapter 5

Making the Sale, Keeping the Customer

I WORE the sales rep's hat – along with the inventor's hat, the marketer's hat, and several other hats – during the start-up years of my business, and Sue wore the rest. At the beginning, we couldn't afford to pay a professional salesperson and wouldn't have even known how to hire one. More importantly, I'd have been reluctant to hand over such critical responsibilities to anyone else anyway. So, despite lacking sales experience or any particular aptitude, I jumped in wholeheartedly as the 'face' of my product. All along, I was being driven by an unflinching belief in my creasing device. I just knew that everyone would want it; they just didn't know it yet.

Seeing Really Is Believing

When I set out to sell my device directly to printing companies outside of the initial wave of easy converts, I quickly learned that some shop owners and managers were sceptical about my product – in the same way that the equipment manufacturers I'd tried to sell my idea to outright had been. Sure, their eyes would light up when I told them my device eliminated the need to outsource creasing.

They would nod in appreciation when I explained how easy my device was to pair with their existing folding machines. Even when I assured them that my Tri-Creaser would pay for itself within two or three job runs, I could almost hear their minds calculating the money they'd save by not having to outsource. All those positives, yet they still didn't commit...

Why was this?

To me it seemed simple: Nobody would believe that my device could produce the results I claimed it could, unless they saw the Tri-Creaser in action.

My challenge, then, was to erode their scepticism sufficiently so that they'd at least let me demonstrate the product on their premises. And that was no small challenge. But I instinctively found a way to whittle away at their resistance: I spoke to their pain.

After all, if something hurts badly enough, people will do almost anything to address the problem that's causing it. And cracking on the fold represented a source of enormous pain throughout the printing industry. I just had to shine a light on it by reminding prospective customers of the poor finishing results, production bottlenecks, increased costs, lost business – and all the immense frustration caused by not having an in-line solution to this problem. It was like prodding someone's tooth as a reminder that they have a toothache – and it worked brilliantly in getting them to open up and let me in.

Once my foot was in the door, I only had to show them the ease and speed with which the Tri-Creaser produced one perfect crease after another. Sceptics quickly became customers. In some cases I was able to sell one or more devices on the spot. And most of those who didn't purchase straight away became customers soon enough – usually when they realised that their competitors were attracting print jobs and earning associated profits that could have been theirs.

Keen to address the "seeing is believing" barrier that was the key to new customers, after six months of hand selling my product, we decided to start selling primarily by direct mail. To that end I presented them with evidence that they could hold in their hand. I created a mailer made out of dark-blue heavy paper stock, featuring an actual crease made with the Tri-Creaser alongside a traditional score made by a standard device. Large type invited the recipient to fold the paper along each indented line and to compare the two results. The evidence was there on the page, plain as day. The fold produced with the traditional scoring device inevitably cracked, while the fold produced by the Tri-Creaser was perfectly smooth. The difference couldn't be ignored and this 'interactive' mailer perfectly demonstrated the Tri-Creaser's capabilities, without the need for an in-person sales call. A lot of leads were generated as result.

Still, I estimated that 95 per cent of the people that were interested or curious enough to call fully expected the Tri-Creaser to fail when put to the test. I even received feedback from some respondents who suggested that, actually, we had cheated on the crease made by the Tri-Creaser! So, thereafter, whenever a prospective customer called, I would simply prod their conscience enough for them to ask themselves that important question: *What have I got to lose?*

I'd remind them that the Tri-Creaser would pay for itself in two or three print jobs, as stated in the customer testimonials in the mailer. I'd then say the Tri-Creaser would take just two minutes to install and then a further two minutes to take off the machine, and if it failed to meet the standards I'd promised, the disturbance to their day would be minimal. I'd answered their question for them: they had nothing whatsoever to lose.

An effective tactic that I often used was to tell

the potential buyer that a printing company around the corner or across town had just bought isometric-Creasers. It was never a lie or an exaggeration. And in most cases the very suggestion that a competitor might have an edge on them was usually enough to convince the owner or manager to take up a demonstration at the very least – which almost always guaranteed another sale. For those who were more difficult to convince, sometimes I would mention that Heidelberg purchased a supply of Tri-Creasers every month to sell along with their folding machines. Just hearing that an industry leader had faith in the Tri-Creaser lent considerable credibility to my product and my company, and often helped to boost my success rate further.

A free two-week trial was a strategy Sue and I devised to appease those who balked at our payment upfront policy. On paper it seemed like a good solution, but in practice it failed because, for one reason or another, some of the companies either didn't return the product after two weeks or didn't place an order. The reasons given were fairly standard for people reluctant to commit to something, to *anything*—they needed more time because an operator was on holiday or they hadn't had any jobs with heavy stock. Or a whole host of other reasons... In the end I ended up spending too much time chasing non-payers, so we did away with the free trials altogether.

A strategy that did work very well in terms of both countering scepticism about my product's capabilities and objection to our payment terms, was our 5 tiered money back guarantee, which was printed on quality gold parchment paper in neat A4 format as part of our free information pack.

The assurance of a full refund if the Tri-Creaser didn't meet their satisfaction within the first three months of purchase, took the risk out of buying a first-of-its-kind product— and that security worked like a charm in turning doubters into customers. Our 5th (last) guarantee stated that our customer could even receive a full refund after 12 months if their Tri-Creaser hadn't saved at least five times more than the cost they paid for it. To this day, our money-back guarantee is a strong selling tool that sets us apart from competitors.

> *"If you show people the problems and show people the solutions, they will be moved to act."* — Bill Gates

How Not Being A Salesperson Actually Helped

During my first ten years of running the business, I never took a sales training course or even attended a seminar, watched a video, or read a book on how to succeed in sales. All I'd done was listen to Steve Hackney, who included elements of it to compliment his marketing strategies. To this day, we have never hired someone with specific sales training or practical sales experience to sell Tech-ni-Fold products. But I have myself been on the receiving end of numerous salespeople—many of whom taught me what *not* to do, and some of whom showed me a better way to attract sales.

Answering the phone or door to a salesperson asking if I'm having a nice day or how I'm doing is a complete turn-off to me. False friendliness doesn't warm me up; it leaves me cold. I can sense straightaway when I'm about to get a pitch for something I don't need or want. Typically, this type of sales rep launches into a tick list of why their product is the answer to my problem – without first making any effort to determine whether I have *any* need for or want what they're selling. Such presumption is off-putting and, ultimately, ineffective. Rather than piquing my interest, it makes me put up my guard because it indicates that the sales rep has no real interest in me, or my needs.

I'm also turned off by salespeople who try to tell me what's best for me or my business, who interrupt and talk over me, who dismiss my objections, or who won't take no for an answer. Such bullying tactics might work some of the time with some people. But they never work on me. And I suspect they rarely work beyond the initial sale, in terms of repeat business and referrals.

Instead I respond more positively to salespeople who go *against* convention—who seek to make a *personal connection* rather than a quick sale. Even though we both know that a sale is the ultimate aim, this subtle difference in approach makes a world of difference in the initial stages of a negotiation. These people know how important it is to focus on building win-win partnerships with their customers, and as such they are usually a pleasure to do business with.

Interestingly, some of the best salespeople I know are in print advertising. When they call, we spend a few minutes catching up on what's going on in my business and in the print industry generally. When they ask whether I'm interested in advertising, if my answer is "No thanks" or "Not now," they don't pressure me. When the time is right, I definitely will. And because of the relationship we have created, they know that too.

On the whole I have a good rapport with these sales reps, and they have been very generous in sharing their extensive knowledge of both advertising and the print industry with me. I can call them at any time, even if only to ask a question or a favour, such as for a contact name at a company I'd like to connect with. They're always happy to help, and they don't then ask, "Hey, will you advertise with us this month?" When I do call to advertise, they always guide me toward the right solution for my needs.

With retrospect, the salesperson who influenced me the most was my father. My dad's first sales job was collecting donations for the kidney foundation in the evenings to supplement his day job at the local hosiery factory. He did what he had to do with four children to feed and he took pride in doing it well, When I was around four years old, he landed a job selling insurance and quit the factory. He progressed quickly and became the top-selling agent in the East Midlands region. My mum told me that Dad was wonderful with his customers, warm and genuine. Seemingly, he was a good listener and always put his customers' interests first. Even at an early age, I felt proud of him.

We take a similar approach with our prospects and customers. Like a doctor to his patient, we always listen first. We invite the person we're talking with to tell us about whatever is giving them grief. We ask questions to better understand their situation. Once we're clear on what they need and want, we offer our solution and explain how it will help them to resolve their problem or meet their objective.

If they have questions or concerns, we do our best to address those, and we're always 100 per cent honest. We don't exaggerate what we can do for them or promise something we're not sure we can deliver. In fact, if anything I like it that we under-promise and over-deliver.

If I detect that a customer doesn't need or isn't ready to buy my product yet, instead of trying to lever them in my direction, I'll concede that my product won't benefit them at that time. Then, I ask if we can keep them on our mailing list. Most take me up on that offer, and many become customers when the time is right.

If A Potential Customer Isn't Ready, Willing, Or Able To Buy Your Product, Step Back And Stay In Touch

Just because your product doesn't suit their needs or wants today doesn't mean it won't in the future. When that day comes, you'll be more likely to get their business if you've kept the lines of communication open and flowing.

We've been pleased with and fortunate to have the people on our sales team – all of whom have consistently demonstrated the qualities I find most desirable in a salesperson. The first person we hired to help with sales was Paul Barrett, in 2002. I'd worked with Paul at Senator Print Finishers, where he was a technical specialist. We first brought him into Tech-ni-Fold to assist me in product development, and after two years, he took over the U.K. sales so I could focus on international sales. Paul was enthusiastic about our products, and he had technical expertise to go with it – in addition to a great work ethic, and a positive attitude. As it turned out, he also had a natural aptitude to *sell*. His passion was electric, and his ability to engage customers was extraordinary. Paul helped us out at trade shows, and when he talked about our products with visitors to our booth, it was like listening to an enthusiastic child telling his mum about a new toy. Our customers loved him.

After thriving as our national sales technician for about seven years, Paul asked to return to working exclusively in product development, and we offered his sales position to Lee White. Lee was very nervous as to whether he could pull it off, but we had confidence in him. He had worked in our stockroom for over two years, and he'd been out with Paul on a handful of product demonstrations. Lee also had experience in manufacturing our products, having previously worked at an engineering company to which we outsourced production. So we threw down the challenge and gave him all the support he needed. We set a sales target, which intimidated him at first, but it didn't take long before he began to exceed it. After a few months of generating strong sales, Lee also started to help train our distributors on how to sell Tech-ni-Fold products, and he became skilled and successful on both fronts.

Most of our international sales come through our distributors, the most successful of which have taken a similar approach to sales as we do at the corporate level, thanks to our personal input and support. They focus on providing solutions and on building long-term relationships with customers. They're sounding boards for the people who buy and use our products – and they use their technical expertise to guide the customer on how our products can help them.

In contrast, my typical experience with sales reps who tried to sell equipment to me during my time working for print-finishing companies was that they would turn up by appointment, smiling and looking business-like in their smart suits, but not knowing anything about how to operate the machines they were selling.

Those types of salespeople might have taken us to their showrooms or treated us to lunch, but they talked as much, if not more, about football or some other side topics than they ever did about the product they wanted us to buy. Their approach didn't seem genuine, and their presentation usually didn't give us the information or the level of confidence in the product we needed to purchase the machine in question.

For Tech-ni-fold products, technical expertise is essential for front-end selling. Some of our team members lack the technical knowledge required for that discipline, but they know and can articulate the main features and benefits of our products. They also know when to hand over a prospect or customer to someone who does have technical expertise. We always encourage our support staff and new distributors to listen in when one of our more senior sales technicians is discussing or demonstrating our products.

I still love observing Paul as he describes and demonstrates our products. His eyes sparkle as brightly and his pride burns as strongly as the day he first presented them. His enthusiasm is infectious, and watching it spread to his captivated audience is magical. You just can't train someone to do that. It comes straight from their passion for what they are selling and for how it will benefit the customer.

In general, people tend to buy from someone with whom they feel personal connection and whom they feel has their best interests at heart. It is not unusual for me – or one of our sales team – to spend 30 minutes chatting with a customer or prospect about their daily work and the challenges they're dealing with. Then, when it's our turn to speak, they listen and they trust us – knowing that our aim is to make their pain go away or to enable them to achieve their goal. If we can help, we explain exactly how.

It's a natural process of seeking to understand a problem and then communicating how we can help to solve it. It's a basic approach that's often overlooked nowadays. With us there is no hard sell and no pressure to "close" the sale. We know that if they book an on-site product demo, or see us at a trade show, or watch one of our videos, or hear about us from a colleague, or read one of our white papers or marketing pieces, a sale often follows anyway.

Looking back, I think the reason having zero sales expertise has worked in our favour is because we've always brought an abundance of empathy, curiosity, knowledge, integrity, and enthusiasm to the goal of helping out, rather than selling to, our customers. It's a subtle difference, but an important one.

> *"Enchantment is the purest form of sales. Enchantment is all about changing people's hearts, minds, and actions because you provide them a vision or a way to do things better. The difference between enchantment and simple sales is that with enchantment you have the other person's best interests at heart, too."* — Guy Kawasaki

From Cold-Calling To Sales Consulting

During my first twelve months or so in business, before the mail-order system was in full flight, a good portion of our sales came from cold-calling prospects I'd pin-pointed in business directories. Consequently, I spent every spare hour after my day job, driving far and wide to show print managers and finishers what I had developed to make their working lives easier. On weekday holidays, I would get up at 4:00 am to head to London with a case of Tri-Creasers – and I'd challenge myself not to come back until I'd sold them all.

I hated cold calling, but back then it worked amazingly well for me – in large part because I didn't take the conventional route of targeting the primary purchasing agent. Instead, I took advantage of the way most print companies are set up – with the office and the factory set apart like two separate worlds in which "the guys in the ties don't mix too much with the lot in the shop." I would turn up at a big printing company and enter through the back door of the factory an hour or so before the office staff arrived. That way, I could avoid being sent packing by the gatekeepers and could chat with the early-shift workers in the shop.

Even though I strolled into the shop like a stranger off the street, I spoke their language and could usually strike up a conversation with one of the print finishers or the print-finishing manager. The fact that I had walked in their shoes put them at ease, and we inevitably got into a discussion about whatever problems they were having – which often included exactly the problem my device eliminated.

When I chose to cold-call by phone, I'd ring between 6:15 and 8:45 in the morning knowing the call would be picked up by someone in the factory since the office would likely not yet be open. The forklift driver or dispatcher or whoever answered the phone would fetch the print-finishing manager or lead operator. As with my drop-in visits, I'd strike up a conversation about some aspect of the trade, and we'd end up talking about whatever struggles they were going through. By the time I told them the purpose of my call, they regarded me not as a salesman but as a down-to-earth guy, just like them, who'd come up with an idea to make their lives easier.

Sometimes the print-finishing managers didn't have the authority to buy, and they would hand me over to the production manager or company owner. Owners, in particular, seemed to find it surreal to see someone like their finishing manager sitting before them in a suit and tie – making the audacious claim of having invented a device that would improve the quality of their work. Many were intrigued with the idea of me being an inventor at all. They would smile when I told them about my ups and downs in bringing my product to market and about my exploits in landing a deal with Heidelberg.

Regardless of whomever I spoke to though, when I cut to the chase and told them I had developed a solution that would take away their cracking on the fold headache forever, they all thought I was crazy. But still, because of my soft approach and human backstory, most of them liked and respected me enough to give me the opportunity to demonstrate my product. And even if I didn't book a product demo or sell any devices that day, I usually left feeling like I'd at least made a good impression and a valuable connection. Ultimately, a good many of them bought my device and also put in a good word for me. So, as much as I detested cold calling, it was always well worth it.

Cold calling is an art form, and none of us at Tech-ni-Fold are fond of or especially good at it. I did it in the beginning because I had no choice. I needed to generate income to put food in the mouths of my family, literally, and also because I had no brand recognition in the market. My early success with cold calling came partly from that desperation and partly because I was forced into grabbing the low-hanging fruit.

The truth is, certain people love being the first to try something new, and some are drawn to the idea of buying from long-shot little guy. My story of trying to break out of the factory and change my life resonated with the people who gave me that shot early on, and on some level they wanted to be part of my success. I think they were secretly hoping that "one of their own" had hit the jackpot.

Those early customers continued to root for me over the years, and many still do. Most went on to purchase enhanced models of the Tri-Creaser and my subsequent inventions. Their leap of faith in me helped to build credibility in the market. And then, after about four years of good practice, our reputation went before us. By then, the majority of our sales came from more efficient and cost-effective methods of selling our products, such as direct mail and online. Consequently, cold calling and hand selling became a rarely exercised choice rather than a necessity.

These days though, it's all about getting the right messages to the right people so that they come to us. As such, most of our sales are made with little or no customer interaction. When we do need to work harder for the sale, we hone in on what the customer is struggling with and then guide them to the right solution – even if that means recommending a competitor's alternative.

I wouldn't have a clue how to sell a product if I didn't know exactly how it would benefit the customer. And I wouldn't attempt to sell a product that I knew the customer didn't need or want. Neither would anyone else on our sales team or our distributorship.

Essentially, we function as consultants rather than as closers, and that approach has worked very well for us. We usually get the order without even having to ask for it, and 90 per cent of our customers give us repeat business.

> *"To sell is above all to master the art and science of listening."* — Tom Peters

Selling Quality

As simple as my invention might have looked to some, I *knew* it was worth its weight in gold to my target market. That knowledge gave me complete confidence and belief and I focused on specifically selling the quality of my solution – that is, its value to prospective customers.

That is not the approach most commonly taken by companies or individuals selling products. When pitching their creations to potential buyers, inventors and innovators tend to focus on what their product is and what it costs – rather than on what it is *worth* to the customer. Inventors are not alone in their tendency to focus on *what* they're selling rather than on *why* the customer should buy it. So do many early-stage entrepreneurs and even professional salespeople.

In my experience, selling quality is an effective approach with 90 to 95 per cent of buyers. The other 5 to 10 per cent will happily trade quality for cost. We sometimes receive calls from prospects that object to paying more for our device than for a competitive solution of inferior quality. We politely listen as they blow off steam, and then we try to point out the benefits of our product, but even that rarely works. When someone puts price over quality, there is usually nothing that can be done to change their perspective.

Unfortunately, bargain hunters sometimes fall prey to fly-by-nights – like the one who got under my skin at a major trade show. This person had been selling his scoring device out of the boot of his car, claiming it worked better than the Tri-Creaser and cost half as much. Now, here he was in my booth, strolling around like he owned it. Then, he approached me with a smug smile and boasted that he didn't need to pay to exhibit because he was signing up customers by going from stand to stand. I'd spoken with him previously and had always dealt with his animosity toward me in a professional manner. This time, I lost my cool.

I told him I'd worked hard to build my company and to conduct business in an honest fashion – as had all the manufacturers at the show that had invested in showcasing their latest technology. I told him that people like him – who roam exhibition floors to drum up cheap business for their inferior products – couldn't be taken seriously and wouldn't be long in business. I rarely get irate; I'd done so only once before in sixteen years, with the gatekeeper at MBO America. But I was fed up with this guy mocking me and misrepresenting himself in the market. Not just that, many of his customers were confused about who his supplier actually was and mistakenly thought he was selling Tri-Creasers – all of which was having a negative effect on our reputation.

Not surprisingly, this guy had no after-sales strategy to speak of. He certainly didn't go back to fix problems with his device or to replace it when it failed to perform as he'd promised – nor did he supply consumable parts. He was just a chancer whose sole aim was to make a quick profit. Fortunately, many of his customers ended up calling us to replace his devices with Tri-Creasers anyway.

Sadly – and this applies in any market for any goods – there will always be those customers who are unwilling or unable to pay more for the higher-quality products in the market. In my opinion, it is a mistake to undercut your price or to spend excessive time trying to change their minds. Instead, I think it's better to channel your efforts on selling quality to those who want the best value rather than the lowest price.

Making Our Customers Love Us

As well oiled and effective as our direct-response sales system was, we occasionally had to work hard to get our products into a major print firm. That meant giving them special attention, doing on-site product demonstrations, and making several follow-up visits to their site. That was all part of the package.

Likewise, we sometimes had to handhold a new customer until they got a grip on our product or to go and fix a problem for them. For instance, early on, a few new customers complained of results that fell short of their expectations, and although I knew it was probably down to their operators having made setting errors, as an act of good faith I travelled to their site to fix the problem free of charge anyway

Once, after making the three-hour drive to one of these customers, I was greeted with silence by the disgruntled operator who had called in the complaint. It took me all of two minutes to reset the pressure on the folding machine's shafts to which my device was attached. And when I turned on the machine, the Tri-Creaser did its job – churning out nice deep creases that didn't crack when folded. The rather sheepish operator (who should really have checked and adjusted the setting himself) fetched me a cup of coffee by way of apology, and I made the long journey back.

But that exercise wasn't wasted time. It was an opportunity in that it prompted me to include a troubleshooting tip in our next customer newsletter about checking and adjusting the pressure settings on folding machines. If nothing else, including that information might have prevented further similar trips.

Business went along like that for some time, with very few and only minor customer complaints – all of which could be resolved by giving advice over the phone or visiting the customer to adjust a setting. Then, I took a phone call from the managing director of a small print shop in London, reporting that one of the settings on his Tri-Creaser was randomly damaging the paper he was creasing. After quizzing him on the specifics, I learned that the damage only occurred every 50 to 60 millimetres. This indicated to me that something on a specific area of either the rubber component or the metal channel beneath it was causing the abrasion. I hadn't come across this problem before, and to say I was worried is an understatement.

While I tried to get to the bottom of the problem, three other customers called with the same complaint. All my self-doubts came rushing back...

Was I just lucky in selling a few hundred devices?

Would more calls of this nature follow?

Was the problem restricted to certain types of

paper stock, or was my device defective?

Was it a manufacturing glitch or a flaw in my design?

While allowing this glitch to make me momentarily doubt my creation, I also worked out that all of the Tri-Creasers in question had been made in the same batch of twenty. So I visited each of the customers who had called to report the problem in turn, and upon examining their devices; I discovered the same manufacturing defect in every offending device. I went to the engineer I was using at the time and said, "What's happening? Can you find out what's causing this?"

As it turned out, what was happening was that, with use, the tools were becoming blunt whereupon a barely visible nick was developing in the channel at exactly the same place – in this case between 50 and 60 millimetres.

I replaced all of the defective devices in that batch of twenty, including those of customers who had not even called to report a problem, with new Tri-Creasers. Of course, I first inspected each replacement device and tested them on the same stocks that had been damaged at the customer sites to ensure they performed flawlessly.

Despite the odd unforeseen glitch, our products have improved and evolved through innovation, and customer complaints are very rare. When the rare problem does arise, fixing it quickly and fully is our first priority, and we continue to provide a full money-back guarantee on all of our products. We also still offer free product demonstrations and installations, while most other suppliers charge by the expensive hour for those services.

Sue and I believe with a passion that customer

dedication doesn't end once the sale is made and the product is received. Nor is it limited to reacting to customer complaints. It also means being proactive by periodically reaching out to our customers to ask how things are going and to offer our help. Our goal is not to merely satisfy customers; we want to make customers love us.

In the beginning, I would ring each new customer about a month after the sale to ask how they were getting on, half-expecting them to tell me the device didn't work, or that its rubber component had burnt up, or that something I hadn't thought of had gone wrong. Instead, almost all of my customers raved about the Tri-Creaser, often telling me it had paid for itself within two or three weeks. After two years of personally calling every new customer, we switched to sending out personalized letters thanking the customer for their purchase and offering our assistance in helping them to make the most of their device. But, one way or another, we wanted customers to know that we are always there.

Nowadays, we check-in on existing customers too from time to time. But now that we have tens of thousands of customers, it is obviously a little more difficult to communicate with each one on an individual and more personal basis. So, while we will occasionally ring up a customer, send a personal note, or drop by for a visit, much of our customer outreach is done via mass email.

One of our most welcomed e-notices – which always results in good dialogues with customers and a bump up in sales – is our annual offer for a free "health check" to identify and address any operation or quality issues with our products. Sometimes, we offer free product-enhancing upgrades, too. We also use newsletters, e-blasts, and social media to share industry news, print-finishing, updates on product enhancements and new products, stories about our customers, and links to videos and articles that might be helpful to our customers.

Trade shows are another great way to connect with customers. We offer free trade show tickets to our customers, and we go to great lengths to welcome both customers and prospects to our booth. We're always prepared to address their concerns, answer their questions, listen to their suggestions, and discuss how our solutions can make their lives easier and the quality of their finished work better.

Even though much of our communication with prospects and customers is conducted via the Internet, they always have the option of talking with a real person over the phone. In fact, our customers know that they can pick up the phone and speak to us anytime, not only about our products but also about any aspect of printing. Our sales support and customer service team members are fantastic with our customers – always friendly, courteous, and responsive. They make sure questions get answered, problems get solved, information packets get sent, and products get delivered – accurately and expediently.

To ensure our ability to fill orders quickly and efficiently, we streamlined our worldwide distribution operation and keep up to £1 million worth of stock on hand. That goes against the grain of most suppliers in our industry. Few manufacturers of printing equipment hold so much stock, and customers usually have to wait a few weeks for their orders because of that. We can usually ship an order the day it is received and ensure delivery within three working days. We have even sent motorcycle couriers to make some deliveries. New customers are shocked by our fast turnaround, and all of our customers appreciate and rely on this added benefit of our solution. You need to go beyond the call of duty in order to impress your customers and stay ahead. That requires consistently delivering not only a quality product but also quality service.

Our customers welcome our calls, too. Sometimes I'll phone a few select customers to let them know about a new product or an upgrade that I think might benefit them. I still like to ring up our best customers just to chat or to talk about an issue or trend in our industry. It's amazing how much I learn from them. In fact, their feedback and input have been invaluable to us in improving our products and developing new solutions.

Going the extra distance to keep our customers happy and in the loop has paid off in dividends – as evidenced by their loyalty and repeat sales.

> *"The best customer service is if the customer doesn't need to call you, doesn't need to talk with you. It just works."*
> — Jeff Bezos

Many inventors and innovators treat their work strictly as a creative endeavour, too often at the cost of its commercial success. They get caught up in developing their product and tinker for perfection, but perfection never comes and even a small improvement can take months to achieve. They put off trying to sell their products, claiming they're "not good at sales" and waiting for an investor to provide the capital to hire a professional salesperson. But going months or years without a pay cheque while spending money on proto-types and patent fees is a booby trap that lies in wait.

I cannot emphasize enough the importance of inventors getting out there, in person, and selling their inventions. Who better to sell a product than the person who created it – the person who knows how it works, how it benefits the customer, and how it stacks up against the competition? The product doesn't need to be perfect; it needs only to be sufficiently better than existing solutions. That's the tipping point at which an inventor needs to start selling their creation like their livelihood depends on it, because it most likely does.

I'd be lying if I said I wasn't intimidated at the prospect of selling my invention. But not only was it my only option, it was the right one – and don't forget I had the luxury of Sue's invaluable help and advice along the way. I learned a lot about my product, which enabled me to improve it and make it even more enticing and valuable to the market. Even more significantly at that early stage of the game, we started bringing in money within weeks of receiving my patent-registration. In fact, I sold enough during my first year of business to pay back the loan from my sister, pay for our U.K. patents as well as the manufacturing, marketing, and overhead expenses – and make a good profit on top of that.

"Even if you are on the right track, you will get run over if you sit there." — Will Rogers

Chapter 6

The American Dream

ONE OF MY earliest recollections as a child is of my dad playing Frank Sinatra records –specifically the song 'New York, New York'. Although I had no way of processing its 'if you can make it here, you can make it anywhere' message in terms of what it might mean to my future business ventures back then, part of me, on a very simplistic level at least, could identify with what the song was saying.

Like most people, I grew up with my own impression of what the so-called American Dream was. At the very least I knew that the U.S.A. seemed to offer life-changing opportunity for anyone that dared to believe. As I got older, into my teenage years, that belief was reinforced – probably by way of exposure to movies and popular culture in general – by an idealistic sense that, regardless of ethnicity, education or background, the American Dream was available to anyone. Furthermore, I was attracted to the fact that young Americans grew up in the knowledge that this promise of prosperity was actively *encouraged* – even if the odds of achieving it were, in reality, quite remote.

From my remote position in England, I admired the philosophy that suggested people really could beat the odds – particularly because it was becoming increasingly apparent that the British way was radically different. We seemed to relish the process of building heroes up, only to knock them down to where they came from later. The concept of failure seemed to be an admirable stepping stone to success in America, whereas the idea of 'once a failure, always a failure' seemed to ring true in the U.K.

Fast-forwarding many years later to when I was contemplating capturing some of the American Dream for my company, I was adamant that making a sizeable impression across the Atlantic shouldn't be restricted to making it in New York. Even I knew that it was just the symbol, the touchstone for prosperity – and I'd heard enough stories about companies making their fortunes in this huge land of dreams to realise that if I wanted any part of it, I'd need to launch a broad, well-thought-out offensive on the North American market as a whole. These success stories only inspired me to find a way to break through.

To that end, finding a good reseller in the states was always my biggest goal from the start. It was reassuring and inspiring to consider that the print market in the states was at least eight times bigger than its U.K. equivalent. I knew without a shred of doubt that my product had the potential to sell on a massive global scale. But the secret was in trying to find and to convince the right people with a similar background to me, to take that step up to promote and sell the products in their own country, under a lucrative contract of exclusivity.

You would think this would be easy, wouldn't you?

However, there are many factors that work against such a potentially lucrative business arrangement from ever seeing the light of day – not least that question of authenticity in terms of whether the claims of some former print finisher in England really held true when it came to solving a major industry problem that was generally considered to be "unsolvable." Even now I have issues convincing people in one country that my product solved the problem in many others. Those people in one country who, upon hearing that my product solved the problem in many others, were still unwilling to even part believe in that possibility no matter how we try to convince them, were an enduring challenge.

As it turned out, I would live the American Dream vicariously through a couple, Andre and Gina Palko, who became the first U.S. resellers of my products. My method for finding someone like Andre Palko dated back to the incredible learning process I went through, which began the day when Steve Hackney first knocked on our door.

Without any doubt, it was Steve who equipped me with a proven toolkit of effective and powerful sales and marketing strategies. Steve and I met at exactly the right moment in our respective lives. It was the perfect storm of innovator and marketing genius, cutting their teeth together for what was coming down the line. It truly was a surreal meeting of minds. In a nutshell, Steve's expertise gave me the ability to bring an unproven, relatively unheard of solution to the U.S. print market, and later, far beyond. After he'd helped me open up the U.K market, it made total sense to trust in his method thereafter.

As I've alluded to, the absolute key to everything was to turn scepticism into believing customers, and that required convincing potential business partners and resellers to adopt our proven business model for themselves. With it we sold a *lifestyle*, not just a dry business opportunity. There's a huge difference. A lifestyle is tangible and drives a fundamental desire for change. A business opportunity, if not accompanied by anything else, is just numbers on a page. I'd even go a stage further and say that we sold a *dream* lifestyle and the promise of wealth to would-be entrepreneurs, offering the benefits it would bring to those who just believed. Then, if they believed and took our advice, it came true. The premise really was as simple as that.

To present the opportunity effectively, we developed a step-by-step roadmap to success for those willing to take instruction and have the faith to know that it would work. The most difficult part was finding the right type of people. Steve knew that I had previously been drawn to the idea of getting in with the big hitters who dominated markets, and, significantly, he knew that such relationships would ultimately fall flat. He had seen it all before: dealerships trying out the latest thing only to refocus on more profitable products of larger magnitude once the novelty wore off (and ditching the inventor at a moment's notice). That had already happened to me more than I care to remember, most painfully with MBO and Baumfolder in the U.S. Instead, Steve wanted to target individuals similar to me who had the passion to grow something into a life changing enterprise – who respected and understood the potential of such a business model, and who might therefore replicate my success in their own country.

At the outset, I won't deny that I did feel uncomfortable with so blatantly pitching this business model dressed up so garishly in the promise of wealth and the concept of making dreams come true for the right person. But it really wasn't a lie. In every case where our trust and instructions are adhered to (and sometimes complemented with the new partner's ideas) life changing wealth has followed.

As it turned out, when I placed the free advertisement on a U.S. website in 2002, there was only one response: Andre. When I initially received his email I was a little puzzled as to how he'd ever found out about my company. At that point I'd forgotten I'd even placed the ad. But the fact that he even made contact felt like fate from the start. And then when I heard more about Andre's background, I was even more convinced that I'd found the right man.

In many ways Andre was a mirror image of me. He'd spent twenty years working for other people in the print finishing business. He was diligent and excellent at his job, but deep inside he thought he was capable of so much more. He'd just never taken that kind of leap of faith that I was now presenting him with. He openly admits that when he saw the advertisement and spoke to me on the phone shortly afterwards, he was sceptical. But as I've said, our pitch and approach was designed to overcome that, and that included sending Andre a Tri-creaser to trial without any obligation whatsoever. For some reason I felt comfortable with the idea of trusting in him, and that extended to the act of actually investing some of my product with him.

Trust Is A Two-Way Street

Ultimately, the truth is that – to make a long distance business arrangement work – two people need to take a leap of faith to some extent. Fortunately, both Andre and I were receptive to that. Sure, I spent hours speaking to him by phone to develop the relationship over a period of time – primarily to get a firm picture of the man who'd essentially be our business face in the U.S. As we spoke in greater depth, I could feel the passion and hunger he clearly felt about creating a business selling my products, and he had all the knowledge and experience I could ever wish for in a person.

Along the way, I gleaned two further pieces of information that seemed significant. Firstly, I felt that Andre was probably earning the equivalent type of wage that I used to as a print finisher a few years prior to our conversations. While this was probably decent, it was also quite likely to be below his desired expectation. In my mind it felt like we might at least be talking the same language. Secondly, I sensed that he was supporting his wife Gina in getting her through college and that money was really tight. Consequently, he was hungry for the opportunity that I needed him to seize to make the deal work for me.

As a result, I found myself making the first step and taking the initial risk. There wasn't a lot to think about. The worst-case scenario for me was that Andre Palko disappeared over the horizon with my Tri-Creaser leaving me on the hook for a few hundred dollars. It was a risk I could easily afford to take. His potential loss by accepting a Tri-Creaser was nil. I was so sure he was the right guy that I didn't even activate the money-back guarantee. I don't feel that kind of comfort every day.

Despite selling the trial unit to a local print shop in the first few days after an in-person demo, Andre understandably felt his way slowly with the Tri-Creaser. As good an opportunity as it was, and as confident as we both were about the strength of the market, Andre and Gina (who worked tirelessly on a part-time basis) weren't in any position to get into a situation whereby they were sitting with stock that they couldn't afford to pay for after thirty days. Nevertheless, using Andre's contacts combined with Gina's amazing selling skills, a wealth of acquired marketing strategies and new leads generated at a print industry show, they managed to sell the initial order of forty units he had on invoice. Andre then placed another order for more Tri-Creasers.

Thereafter he decided, like I had many years previously, to devote all his time to selling the product, utilising the skills, resources and support of his wife on a part-time basis. As it was in my case, removing the safety net of an existing job that brought in a guaranteed monthly income was a step into the unknown. But again, like I had, Andre saw a better life for him and his family, and it was this drive and vision to make it work that helped him sell the product in these early stages, with Gina on the verge of coming on board full-time.

But this was just the start.

Keen to see how much outreach some solid advertising might have, I suggested that Andre should place a full colour, full-page ad in one of the U.S. print trade magazines. These kinds of ads don't come cheap – but in my mind it was a case of speculating to accumulate. Andre was less positive. He still felt a little sceptical about the possibilities. But I was willing to invest in him again, so I agreed to pay for that first issue in full. I also gave him the template for the ad, so that he could revise and tweak it for future U.S. campaigns.

The results were excellent. Andre's phone, email and fax went into meltdown with leads in response to the advertisement. As he'd done with the trade show leads, he followed up with a letter offering an in-house demo, and as a result he sold a lot of tools. As expensive as the ads were, it was obvious that selling a couple of products would cover the cost, so from that point on I offered to split the cost of monthly advertisements in select U.S. print trade publications that had healthy circulations.

From that point on, Andre's business yielded incredible results. Andre and Gina had set a goal of selling 400 Tri-Creasers in that first year. They did that with time to spare. But their success was only beginning. I wanted to invest in them again...

I invited Andre and Gina over to the U.K to spend some time in our company, on our premises, picking our brains about some of the marketing techniques that we'd been employing for some time already. Again, they had nothing to lose and everything to gain. All he needed to do was get on a plane. They'll both say now that that trip was life changing in terms of the trajectory of his business. And when you consider that their sales tripled the first year thereafter, then doubled again in the next, that wouldn't be an exaggeration.

In fact, by 2008, the U.S. division of the business was named on the Time Inc. 5000 fastest growing companies in the U.S. All he did was apply some of the simple marketing and sales techniques that we had already been using and the customers did the rest. In essence, I asked Andre to believe and he did. He's now reaping the benefits. His life has been transformed like mine was a few years prior. Not just that, he has now taken less of a leading role in the business in the last few years, leaving Gina and her talent in sales to take it to the next level. The Palkos and Tech-ni-Fold U.S.A. is a match made in heaven.

Not everyone is as dedicated and as trusting as Andre Palko was however. I still get a good stream of prospects coming through – people who'd like to work with us. But it never fails to amaze me that so many seemingly "smart" business candidates won't proceed for one reason or another. I've learned through trial and error and experience that it takes a certain type, and you can never really tell until you meet someone face to face. Often I hear that business only requires a certain amount of intelligence and common sense. As controversial as this may sound, I'd say that intelligence is overrated sometimes. Common sense and the ability to follow simple instructions are far more important.

For people willing to take the step, we offer a full, two-day technical and marketing training programme here at our headquarters in England. We look after all the hotels and costs when the candidate lands – but many won't even commit. It seems to me that they want guaranteed income right away, with no risks involved on their end. I understand that many of those that reply might have limited income and they may have those difficult "but what if" or "but what if not" conversations with a spouse or colleague, however, only they can make the final call. Again, as I've said many times, scepticism is the eternal adversary for our solutions. People need to be able to see beyond the doubts.

A Proven Method Just Needs To Be Repeated

We later approached the Mexican market with a similar approach as we had with the U.S. Although there's a language barrier there that complicates things slightly, the basic idea was the same: I just had to find that right individual. And I did. His name is Rodrigo Castellanos.

Like Andre, Rodrigo had experience in the print finishing industry; he'd been working for several years in the family business in Mexico. Also, like Andre, Rodrigo demonstrated to me a level of drive, work ethic and passion that made me think he was the right person to distribute our products in his country. And I would be proven correct in that assessment.

Initially he purchased five of my products for his father's print company. Thereafter he kept emailing me to say thank you for having developed such a great solution. He also mentioned that it was quite an undertaking to convince his family about the worth of the products given the high relative cost of the tools based on the standard of living in Mexico. Yet he still took that step and believed, and I thanked him for doing it. Rodrigo was exactly the right type of person I was looking for. In effect we found each other, and Rodrigo had transformed his life as a result.

Our approach to resellers/distributors has been a significant part of our progress. We have worked with over 100 distributors worldwide and a handful of those are responsible for bringing in most of our business. These people are entrepreneurs – special business people who completely buy into the company values and, by extension, my ethos. Some of them actually started as customers and therefore could see what value our products brought to their company, and some just came across us by seeing adverts or through meeting us at trade shows. These people have become wealthy through selling our products and have built good business enterprises. They all implement the strategies we recommend and all have the good sense to apply their own strengths too. My door will always be open to anyone with that mind-set. If you're reading and that's you, you know what to do...

In addition to these relationships, we also have many more non-exclusive arrangements with dealers and manufacturers, sometimes because that crucial element of belief hasn't been completely alleviated on their side – yet they recognise the value of our products to their customers just enough to warrant stocking them. I view these types of relationships as 'door-openers' in that these companies access business relationships that they otherwise might not, because they are not on the existing supplier list for certain buyers.

For example, one company called me to say that he'd sold a folding and binding system for £250,000 because his customer insisted that our Tri-Creaser must be installed at the heart of any solution. That's good news. In Germany, our distributor, Uwe Reimold became the biggest seller of folding machines there because he led with our Tri-Creaser. Doors opened up to those who purchased competitive folding machines, they'd buy a Tri-Creaser, gain trust in Mr Reimold and when it came to replacing their machine, you can guess what happened? He smashed sales targets. He remains a vital member of the extended team courtesy of his incredible drive paired with his ability to access the major print companies.

Even still, I'm always surprised by how few, relatively speaking, are willing to take a chance in a situation that has basically no downside to them. For example, once I sent out information packs to one hundred dealers in Switzerland. I got just five replies. That still amazes me. What doesn't amaze me is that one of those replies came from a company that entirely bought into our ideas, and have since become a very important cog in the Tech-ni-Fold wheel. They believed, and we all win. When it happens like that, all the hard work is worthwhile and nowadays, as we have a bigger brand, we attract more attention from other manufacturers who see the benefits in our technology and therefore want to work with us.

Relationships like this turn into friendships because they tap into the important values of trust and compromises. Sue has taught me how important cash in the bank is and I am never embarrassed or hesitant in picking up the phone if payment from a distributor is late. They still get the polite version of me, but what I say is direct, concise and clear, and it usually sorts the situation out immediately and this can only be done by being clear about all aspects of the collaboration from day one – including the all important area of payment. This way I think the respect builds by being honest and clear; we simply have to pay our suppliers and our staff.

On some occasions where distributors are late in paying, Sue alerts me and we discuss the reasons, but mostly it leads to a hold on sending out the next order. That's not me being harsh—not at all. I always think that I have done a lot to build up our distributors business by backing the individuals in the early stages. I expect an equal degree of respect the other way and by and large it's there. I don't need to spend my time chasing money – that just undermines the creative process.

In a nutshell the distributor arm of the business spreads the word about the company into territories that we'd struggle to access ourselves without devoting a lot of time and energy that would be better deployed elsewhere. Tech-ni-Fold U.S.A. especially has given us a degree of legitimacy in the eyes of the big industry players that is particularly gratifying for me. It feels satisfying to occasionally get the acceptance, albeit grudging at times, that I didn't initially get when I first came up short in the land of opportunity.

We have, at various times in the past, had almost 100 distributors selling Tech-ni-Fold products worldwide. Recently we have streamlined that list down in order to focus on the more serious collaborations to avoid spreading ourselves too thin. As it stands, we still sell to up to fifty-five distributors but we don't list them all on our website. Many of these are more like good contacts/sales organisations that will call us whenever they find a customer who wants what we can supply. In that respect, they're more passive than active.

Regardless of numbers, we have yet to come up with a territory that comes remotely close to the sales we do in the U.S. Although we do have a reseller in China, the actual sales potential is quite low because of the price. In any case, our distributor targets the more affluent print companies who demand quality. India brings the same kind of issues as China. Our technology is proven and highly sought after (we are never short of approaches) but often, as was the case with Autoprint, distributors want to sell for 75% less than our RRP, and it is very difficult to meet such price points, especially when factoring in any kind of discounts.

We've had various conversations with Indian companies in the past, but they almost always end with them proposing to manufacture in their home country, and then mass selling at reduced margins. The low margins are one thing, but the bigger issue is being sure of what quality of build you're getting, and this is often hard to measure from a distance. To me, it's just not worth compromising the company's reputation for peerless build quality, just for the sake of some mass sales.

As a company, we remain so busy in other markets it is easy not to look too hard at the Asian continent. That said, there's no doubt that the Chinese and Indian markets could both be incredible, if only there was an easier way to do business there. As it stands, in China you can easily find near-perfect replicas of most of the popular brands of print finishing equipment. In fact, I myself was burned there. Ten or so years ago, I found a Chinese company who had copied an early design of a creasing unit I built. The guy was so proud of that when he told me; he thought he was paying me a great compliment! That's what you're dealing with: a different culture altogether, where the risks greatly outweigh the benefits at this time. Maybe one day we'll revisit.

Chapter 7

To Breaking Point

THERE COMES A POINT in the trajectory of any business where the initial excitement of fast development, new relationships and all the associated lifestyle changes, level out. That's inevitable – the exhilarating nature of the pursuit of life-changing innovation is difficult to sustain at the absolute edge. When I look back, I often feel that these first few years were where I performed at my best – possibly because the discipline of creating and developing the ideas played more to my strengths than sitting back and allowing the business to run, albeit that I was always considering new ways in which the business could grow.

To that end, post 2005 was pivotal. It was a period of planned consolidation. My alliance with the mercurial Steve Hackney was nearing its end as we both felt that he'd given us as much as he possibly could. At the outset I remember Steve saying that we'd probably only need him for the first year or eighteen months after set up. As it turned out, he was with us for nearly *five* years – maybe because Steve often enjoyed telling me that, if we ever parted company, it would cost me twice as much to hire him again! He was half-joking, probably, but I knew he was getting busier, and that his fees were rising.

Regardless, I wouldn't deny for a second that Steve really had helped us with some of the key areas of growing the business, although after a certain period of time it became obvious to me that some of the ideas he'd brought with him weren't sparking as much interest as they once had. It seemed like the relationship had reached its natural end and, at the same time, using aspects of some of the marketing genius he had taught us, I wanted to take the business forward in a more 'corporate' direction, for want of a better way of putting it.

One thing I really do regret, and it certainly merits a mention, is that I ended my relationship with Steve by email. Not quite as bad as that story about the musician Phil Collins ending his marriage by fax, but it was close. As soon as I pressed 'send', I regretted it. And I have since apologised profusely for it. I could tell he was hurt, and he had every right to be. He said that he thought we were friends, and that friends should have dealt with such a conversation sitting at a table, face to face.

The truth is – from my end certainly – I didn't quite see Steve as a friend. I respected him and I still do and I know he has become very successful and probably wealthy. But he was always more of a consultant or an associate – that's definitely how he carried himself when he was around us. To us he was a commodity who delivered his world-class services in the interests of improving our business. And he did so in such a highly professional manner that it made it seem like he was on a different level. But I knew very little about him or his life and thought that, given we hadn't spoken to each other for a couple of months, to sever the ties by email would be in keeping with what I thought our relationship was at that point. That turned out to be a misjudgement.

There's no doubt that for a company that has new technology and is struggling with how to market, advertise or sell its business, Steve Hackney is a colossus. He truly is a genius that knows exactly where to apply and how to implement a proven marketing formula.

And it's one that could mesh with almost any business. Looking back, just as I was experiencing scepticism about my products when I met Steve, I felt similarly sceptical about his methods. In the end I put my trust in him (a) because he asked me to and (b) because I was asking my customers to, and he delivered in spades by adding hundreds of thousands of pounds to our annual turnover. I'd got my business off the ground, but he was the shot in the arm that it needed to really start flying.

I'd be lying if I said that I didn't sometimes miss Steve's positivity – as well as occasionally wondering how his marketing strategies might help any new developments that the company has. Thankfully, I met Steve a few years ago at a marketing seminar and we again discussed our collaboration and the way it ended. Again I expressed my deep regret; I wasn't professional in my closure of our working relationship and I repeated my apology. If only time could be reversed.

After Steve left we started to solidify what we had, as well as looking at how we could reinvent ourselves. Inertia – albeit highly profitable inertia – isn't a comfortable place for someone like me – an inventor at heart who's always looking to keep moving forward. I definitely felt that a significant part of our future lay with our distributors, and that meant transferring to them some of the e-commerce elements of our own website. I wanted to pair up with strong overseas partners who could promote and market my products in their country, using e-commerce strategies taken from us. Although an e-commerce approach worked very well in terms of picking off sales globally here and there, we were taught (and also found out via communication with some of them) that customers would rather deal with someone in their own country and that this would inevitably increase total sales significantly.

I also noticed that, during the end of Steve's time with us, a good proportion of those globally located customers wanted someone close to them if possible – particularly when they needed some more consumables, where they'd be incurring shipping charges if they came directly from us. Everything pointed towards the fact that setting up a strong network of distributors allowed us to turn over a healthy profit without doing very much. All we had to do was back the distributors, not compete against them. Over time this would prove to be true.

On a wider basis, there was another burning question gnawing at my inventor brain: where was the print business going?

The answer wouldn't be long in arriving.

A New Age

By 2006, the digital print revolution was really starting to gather steam. As a result, digital printing companies were springing up all over the U.K. and throughout the world, driven by the growing demand for small, customised print runs ranging from as little as one copy to up to five thousand. In response to this obvious market opportunity, I identified a logical access point that would represent another big feather in our company hat. I wanted to develop a creasing machine to solve yet another major industry problem: digital cracking. Put very simply: excess toner from the printing process often lies on the sheet of paper and cracks. Customers don't want that. They want their leaflets, menus, book covers and greetings cards etc. to fold perfectly, without defect.

Then it seemed like fate intervened in response to a need for that market access...

I met one of the owners of a Swiss company called Multigraf at a trade show and we got talking about how we might partner in this area. He knew about our technology and we knew about their quality manufacturing, and so we discussed a scenario whereby they could produce a hand-feed unit with a motor to drive the two shafts. And then we discussed how we could produce the devices to fit onto them. In a nutshell, I wanted him to produce the machines exclusively for collaboration with us. He agreed.

Working with Multigraf had immediate and obvious appeal. We benefitted from the best manufacturing processes in regards to the actual machine build quality and – in combination with the Tech-ni-Fold creasing and micro-perforating devices – the machine soon began to do the job intended. We had helped with the design of the hand-feed version, where a customer could feed as many products as they could, according to how fast they needed output to be. This speed would double what was currently available on other traditional hand feed methods.

At one point, Mutigraf called me in to see their version of friction feed in action. Basically their method to speed up output incorporated a mechanical rubber wheel to bite against a roller shaft. This created enough friction to force a handful of sheets through the unit in an accurate forward motion, one after another. Although it appeared to be a reasonable option for those who required more output, I knew from a lot of experience that friction feeding methods were notorious for marking digital stocks. Sheets would regularly slip, and that led to unsightly scuffing marks. This machine still had these shortcomings, and although it troubled me somewhat I agreed that we would offer the option to our distributors as long as we made it clear from the off that there were limitations.

Soon Andre at Technifold U.S.A. was buying the device in batches of fifty and, in addition, we linked Multigraf to another dealer in the U.K. and they too began selling in large volumes. It was really going great guns – and it was a simple chain of command to manage. We received the orders from Multigraf and they outfitted the machines. It was a smooth stream for us and it was growing very nicely throughout the European market.

After two years, the problems started.

Multigraf wanted to sell the machines to their dealers but didn't run that idea by me first. Suddenly I was in midst of a price war whereby the Multigraf dealers were competing with *our* resellers. It caused a lot of awkward issues. We tried to sort out our differences and should have met over a table to correct any misunderstanding face to face before things got out of hand. However, instead the lines of sensible communication eroded fast – not helped by the fact that we believed that Multigraf were telling their dealers that the price of the machines couldn't come down too much because of Tech-ni-Fold's high device prices. That was a move I took great objection to. What could have been a good business partnership was now turning messy.

It wouldn't be long before I lost trust in Multigraf completely. I felt they were becoming unreasonably greedy. They wanted more sales and didn't appear to be concerned that they were upsetting my distributors in the process. That's how I saw it at least. Something had to give – and it did when we agreed not to continue the partnership. (It should be said that they tried to carry on with a scoring device that they legally developed themselves. Like all others who tried to compete using steel as the main scoring agent, their product eventually failed to match Tri-Creaser quality and receded in the market).

This situation wasn't totally new to me, sadly. I had experienced problems in India where I had gone through a similar scenario where a company, Auto-print, manufactured a machine and we produced the tools. It started well: over one hundred machines were sold in India in no time at all. And then, out of the blue, they started haggling on the price of our tools. As it stood, we were already on a modest share because of the discount. Giving more ground would have made the business partnership untenable.

In the Indian manufacturer's case (and Multigraf's for that matter), they both accepted the original terms and yet, when they got the taste of some success, they chose this area of all areas, Tri-Creaser's tool prices, as a means of reducing the overall number. This attitude really frustrated me – not least because we had already discounted as far as we possibly could. But it also felt as if they'd forgotten that it was our products that made the machines so successful in the first place. I felt they were trying to cheapen my technology for the sake of sales. Looking back, I did everything I could to salvage what were two potentially good business relationships. However, when something goes so fundamentally wrong it's usually only my pride that stops me walking away sooner.

The upshot of these relationships was that the writing was clearly on the wall for me. If we wanted to be truly successful, we needed to manufacture and own our own machine outright – and every aspect of it, rather than entering into any more collaborations that might lead to disagreements over pricing. In any case, rather than cheapening my brand, I wanted to build it up in a way that would do it justice – and for it to become the leading product in the market at entry level. I really believed the gap was wide open to do that. It was my belief that printing companies were almost forced to overspend on creasing machines that they couldn't make full use of, simply because nothing else existed. Now I wanted to give these companies a quality product, an affordable option, but not a cheap one. I also wanted to add in extra flexibility that would allow the machine to do more than just crease.

In a strange kind of a way it had been an easy option for me to work with these two companies, even if it was only to prove to myself that my digital creasing ideas would work. After all, the collaborations were virtually risk-free for us; the costs of design and manufacturing were borne on the shoulders of others. Another company, Agor, in Spain had redesigned one of their machines to accommodate our devices and the Turbo-Creaser tool was quickly in operation. It was a high-speed unit that had a motor and electrics incorporated, and it produced up to 20,000 creased/perforated sheets per hour.

We helped to launch the unit at a trade show in 2008. We gave them free space on our stand and they took in excess of twenty orders straightaway – then saw most of them cancelled as the recession swept through Europe almost, it seemed, while we packed up after the show. Again, the risk and loss wasn't ours. All we lost was the possibility of some of our products being part of those sales. We could easily handle that loss, but it also got me thinking about how I could develop a recession proof solution: a creasing and micro-perforating machine that could work without a motor or pump. Better still, it had to be something that digital print companies could afford in tough times.

The inventor in me kicked in again...

As I mentioned, I was already aware that friction feed methods had something of a bad name – principally because they marked the digital toner and spoiled the result of finished work. But I now had this vision that we would become the first company to resolve this issue. I thought the whole idea through quite methodically, and knew that, just like we proved with rotary creasing, there were many new business start-ups who wouldn't care less what the traditionalists thought or said. All they'd be concerned about was that sheets would come out perfectly creased with no toner scuffing. I didn't want some start-up to develop this product though. I wanted it to be me.

Pushing Hard For Eureka Part II

What followed was an incredibly difficult three year period in our history, that resulted in us investing over £500,000 of our own money to solve yet another major industry problem. If I am honest, I think that I was quite selfish and stubborn during this time and have some regret that I put undue pressure onto the shoulders of Sue, who controlled our finances amazingly well despite my spending sprees.

If it wasn't for the success of the existing Tech-ni-Fold core business, we certainly couldn't have done it. In fact, the new venture was funded using a significant amount of Tech-ni-Fold profits from 2008 - 2011. At the outset I had no idea that it would cost so much money to create the new product, or how much blood and sweat we would pour into the project in the process. All I knew was that I had a vision to create a brand new source of business revenue, specifically aligned to digital print. I badly wanted that new dimension capable of carrying my company through its next phase.

Inevitably, Sue, ever the calm financial counter-balance to my more gung-ho approach, was concerned about the implications all along – especially when, after almost three years, I didn't actually have a solution in my hands. Her concern was completely understandable; I was putting everything on the line in search of another eureka moment. Even Paul, one of the most positive people I know, was concerned that we'd gone through so much heartache and disappointment, again and again, to no avail. Many other people might have given up, but I'm not in the habit of giving up on anything. I had to dig in and really analyse the issues at hand.

As far as I was concerned, print companies had few affordable creasing solutions. A standalone creasing machine would do the job of feeding and creasing awkward digital stocks, but it would also set them back in the region of eight to ten thousand pounds – hardly viable for processing as little as fifty or a hundred sheets a day. These creasing machines used what's called the matrix method where a blade strikes the paper in a channel in pre-determined places that allow a crease or fold to be made. One of the reasons why these machines were so expensive was because a vacuum pump was required to filter air through the sheets with the feeder drum sucking them up individually prior to advancing them to the creasing application.

This vacuum pump system was industry standard in a variety of finishing machines, but I knew that when it came to heavier stocks, its shortcomings became more obvious because the sheets become progressively harder to feed the heavier they get. As a result, many turned to friction feeding methods for the heavier stocks, but that led to the toner marking issues I was also acutely aware of.

To proceed anywhere with a solution, I first had to establish exactly why friction methods marked the toner so badly. To do so I purchased a unit from the U.S.A.; it was one of the leading brands. The person that sold the machine to me told me that it would work without the scuffing problem and I told him that if it did I would come back to him to buy more. Also, if it did, I wouldn't need to develop my own solution.

After some early tests I quickly found that the rubber bands used to pick up the sheets were marking every piece of digital material I tried. Furthermore, the belts used to transport the sheets were marking the rest of the paper. It wasn't looking good. I could see how elusive this solution was potentially going to be. I continued with my research to double check if some of the main European companies had modified their feeders to successfully feed digital materials, and I tested two more. I even invited some U.K. dealers in to try their hand, promising to work with them and buy from them if they could achieve what I wanted.

When they turned up to demo, I remember the whole palaver was quite embarrassing on one occasion. The test products these guys brought over were white envelopes or white data with no print, hence there was no ink to scuff in the first place. And when we put some blue digital material through it started to rub off all over the sheets. Pretty soon the technicians were cleaning belts and changing feed bands – it was all a bit desperate.

Meanwhile I carefully studied the way the sheets travelled, often miss-feeding and slipping, which only exaggerated the scuffing problem. There was no real inertia to the process and the gaps in the feed stack made the sheets hesitate and slip which caused terrible marking. Everything pointed towards failure. During times like these I usually feel excited at the fact that existing solutions don't work – that testing the best technology available and seeing it fail miserably only serves to fuel my passion and show me the potential. Here I think less about the details of an actual solution and more on the opportunity that exists for me the inventor.

Shortly afterwards, in a passing conversation with our German distributor, he told me about a one-man company in Frankfurt that sold really nice friction-feed folding machines. This person was seemingly a disorganised yet clever innovator, and apparently he had designed his friction method differently from others. My distributor friend knew that they fed paper well, but its capabilities with digital stocks were so far unknown. After some fact finding by my distributor on my behalf, word came back to me that this inventor guy had perhaps solved some feeding/scuffing issues after all, so I travelled to see him.

When I got there, I was met with most people's idea of the typical, eccentric inventor. He wore grey overalls and had sundry machine parts scattered all over his workshop. But I liked him; he was a very nice person. It was refreshing to meet someone who resonated with me, who understood and respected what I had done. Our admiration for each other stemmed from the fact that we'd both done some amazing things.

When I saw his feeding technology in action, there was no doubt that it worked better than anything else I'd tried. He had indeed come up with some wonderful ideas, but ultimately, after just a small amount of output, the friction band he was using started clogging up with toner and was marking the sheets. We achieved good results for 100 sheets but thereafter he had to clean his feeder band.

To cut a long story short, this innovator had indeed created the raw beginnings of a creasing machine, and I made the decision to purchase it from him because it was clear that he wasn't geared up for production on the scale that would be required. He kept one of the two units (the 'good' one, apparently) and I was sent off with the one that was barely bolted together!

Meanwhile I found a prototype developer called Vic, in Leicester – and took the unit to his factory where Paul and myself stripped it down and made a better, stronger framework. We then set to work on developing a new feeding mechanism, loosely based on the German innovator's embryonic concept. Initially it failed, so we started again, introducing new elements as we went.

After a lot of trial and error over a period of eighteen months, we settled on a prototype with some promise that incorporated elements that certainly enhanced the feeding mechanism and reduced the marking. There was definitely some hope. However, because of the time spent and the money owed to Vic's company for machine development and drawings, I was feeling an escalating degree of pressure to get real results. Regrettably, when we got the unit back to our development facility and tested it rigorously, we found that the two problems still occurred: slight scuffing and no success when feeding paper. A radical rethink was needed.

Frankenstein's Monster

What followed was a hazy and seemingly endless period of time where I came in to work on many evenings and Paul did some testing at home in his garage. Suffice to say, our wives were not impressed. The project was getting more expensive by the day, not just in monetary terms but in terms of time and health too. Paul and I were really getting beat up trying to crack the problem. Then, one evening, I thought I'd made the breakthrough. I'd looked outside normal parameters and mocked a few things together off the cuff. It worked. I went to bed elated. Then, the next morning when I tried to replicate what I'd done, it failed. I was distraught and thought, "How could it work one minute and not the next?" I got the feeling that this was going to be a frustrating pattern. But we pressed on relentlessly nevertheless.

Paul and I focused on the shape of a specific part we were using and, to cut a long story short, decided to create a flat-angled pad that would press gently on top of the belt, allowing for an open gate for sheets to travel through. Without getting too technical again, we developed a kind of angled arc that helped to fan out the sheets at the stack end – so that the sheets were separated enough for good continuity of feed. We got good results. Things were looking up. Paul then rigged up an obscure adaptation of our ideas in his garage and brought it in to try the next day. We were both really tired but were encouraged by how his prototype worked. There was no visible marking.

By the time we'd achieved some degree of success and had working prototypes, the project was in its third year. These were some of the toughest times and I won't deny that on many occasions I considered pulling the plug on the whole idea. Sue often questioned whether it was all worth it, and whether it was just my pride that was keeping me going. For the first time since I started the business, I felt a real sense of pressure and responsibility on my shoulders.

Regardless, desperate for something to go to market with to recover the huge capital already invested in the development, I decided to allow a Czech manufacturing partner company, Cyklos, to produce some production batches on our behalf. I'd considered all kinds of other production options for this idea that I believed in so much, including taking it to American companies to work on. Whilst this was in motion, we launched two hand-feed units, one motorised (CreaseStream junior) and another with a winding handle (CreaseStream Mini standard) which Tech-ni-Fold U.S.A. also sold direct to customers who wanted a relatively inexpensive, simple product that could be sent directly to them. Both were brought out to offset the escalating costs of the flagship unit that would ultimately be called CreaseStream Plus.

There's A Time For Teamwork

While I love being the sole inventor and have come up with many unique and sellable ideas in that role, I also recognise when I need help and the support of an incredible team around me. Inevitably there are areas related to mechanical and electrical components where people have more expertise than me, and the whole

CreaseStream saga was an area that, in retrospect, I needed other people more than ever.

However it's not just the outside help aspect that being part of a team brings. I also believe that inventors can inspire others within a team to push the boundaries of their understanding, and in doing so reach limits that they thought weren't possible. The relationship works both ways in that respect. Being part of a team creates a degree of positivity that is essential when tackling an issue that most individuals would say can't be solved. Yet, as a team, pulling together, we did it. I had the vision, the drive and the belief in what we were doing, but I didn't have all the knowledge and expertise.

Paul was especially amazing. Not only does he invest a huge amount of time in his work, but he also complements my working practices perfectly by being very methodical in comparison to my tendency to be more radical and off the wall with my approach. Mostly I'm happy to share my ideas, but at other times I won't deny that I prefer to work in secret because I'm embarrassed to think that others might fear that I've lost the plot! But between us, we got there in the end and that's what inventing is all about: the journey, and then the destination in the form of a working product with the potential to generate income.

"None of us is as smart as all of us." — Ken Blanchard

When we finally got the first incarnation of CreaseStream Plus working, business started settling down nicely. We made early sales – not specifically into the digital sector but more in the area where customers needed fast output. Although it wasn't quite the recession-busting solution for small to medium sized digital print companies that I'd hoped it would be (the accessories and aids we supplied with the machine meant that it needed to be priced up as a £10,000 machine), we'd at least made some inroads into parts of the market. Also, as an inventor, I'd in some ways justified three years of toil and expense, if only to myself.

Then we hit problems with the CreaseStream plus. Machines started coming back to us because customers were experiencing issues. The cash flow implications of refunds soon became a huge worry. After a bit of analysis, it seemed to me that users – unless they were trained print finishers – were struggling to master some of the machine's more technical aspects. The evidence was pretty clear. We had installed six machines in the U.K. and all of them were delighted – mostly due to the fact that Paul had been on hand to install the machine and train the staff. However, the same didn't apply to machines that were sold abroad via distributors. Seemingly there were too many technical details and idiosyncrasies for the distributors to pass on and explain to their customers. As a stopgap solution we tried to salvage some of these relationships with customer visits and where we couldn't fix the problem we agreed to take the unit back.

Because the returns on these high-value items were starting to hurt, we even discussed the concept of limiting sales to the U.K., simply so that we could keep an eye on them. With that came the realisation that this machine wasn't for everyone. As I thought about it more, with my inventor's head on, I started having doubts – "Maybe this machine is too complicated?" I started wishing that I could turn the clock back to change a few things.

Simultaneously, a point had arrived where Sue and I had to sit down and discuss the identity and future direction of the CreaseStream business. Neither of us could deny that, because it had taken so long to launch, it was taking some focus away from our proven and successful Tech-ni-Fold business. We knew both could stand alone, but nevertheless we decided to separate the machine side of our operation and make CreaseStream into a dedicated company in its own right. That distinction seemed to make more sense. Furthermore, a separation meant that, if we wanted to sometime down the line, CreaseStream could conceivably be sold in the future as a standalone company – rather than have any sale complicated by its tie-in with Tech-ni-Fold.

After the accountant implemented the separation, we essentially had two companies that served the two main areas of the print market. Tech-ni-Fold was dedicated to mainly the offset market, (although we sold to digital printers too), and CreaseStream would predominantly serve the digital sector. Amid all the hard work and push for solutions, it's sometimes hard to stand back and appreciate what you've achieved as an inventor. But when I thought about the fact that we had created an offshoot company using the original technology, I couldn't help but be excited and proud, given where I'd come from.

Then a major setback occurred.

I developed testicular cancer.

It was strange: leading up to the diagnosis I knew something wasn't right. I was getting tired much more easily and, at times felt like I had no gas in the tank. After I discovered a lump, I went to the doctors' and was prescribed some antibiotics. Perhaps predictably, drugs made no difference. I then went to a major international trade show in Germany where I not only had to exhibit our products, but also had to look after a lot of people, including our own distributors. It was full on. And when I eventually crashed out that night, I was really worried about my health. Regardless, I hid my feelings and we had a successful show. Somehow I got through it.

As soon as I got back I made an appointment to see a specialist consultant and had ultra- sound treatment straightaway. As I recall, the person conducting the tests looked concerned. And from what I could see on his screen, I had every reason to be too. Suddenly, there was urgency. I was told to come straight back to see the consultant that evening; they thought it was serious. And in my mind 'serious' could only mean one thing: cancer. I was frozen with fear and called Sue.

I don't suppose anybody knows how he or she will react to such news until it arrives. But in my case, in an instant, any thoughts about business were gone. All the passion and fight I'd become accustomed to harnessing for the purposes of invention, evaporated in that moment. Nothing seemed to matter other than my family at that time. Somehow I drove home in a daze, locked myself in my house and slumped myself in a seated position in the corner of my lounge. I felt numb and lifeless and didn't know what to do. Although I felt I should have my faith to help me, everything was still too raw, too new. The inner peace I so desperately wanted to feel, had yet to enter my heart and mind.

Then something relatively innocuous happened to jolt me out of my gloom. My phone rang and it was my daughter Sophie on the line. Her car had broken down; she had a flat tyre and was stranded on the roadside somewhere in the Leicestershire countryside. Immediately I jumped up and told her I was on my way; she was my only concern. Fortunately, in the interim, Sophie managed to get to a garage that supplied tyres and I ended up meeting her there to pay the bill. Even that felt great.

Just seeing Sophie was the tonic I needed at the time, but I didn't just blurt my news out at that moment. Instead, I went straight to work where Sue followed me into my office. Sue is very caring and instinctive about my feelings, and comforted and reassured me like no one else could. As business continued around us, we shut ourselves away for a few moments while we sat in my office and she said all the right things – things that made me feel strong and hopeful of a good outcome. Sue was my rock in a time of desperation and uncertainty. Right then I could tell that my family were going to be more important to me than ever. 2012 was going to be a tough year.

Cancer was indeed suspected, and the tests and subsequent operation confirmed it. Before the surgery itself, we assembled as a family for the kind of conversation that nobody ever wants to have. I told Sophie and my son Jack my news. I had rehearsed what I was going to say in advance and stayed strong; I didn't want them to see me upset. Sophie cried and Jack walked out of the room. I think he cried too, but boys don't let on sometimes. Moments later we were all back in the room again. United.

For a while I had thought about protecting them from the news. But I figured that they were old enough – and for me to hide the information wouldn't have really been protecting them at all. It would have been selfish – and they would never have forgiven me. As it stood I felt such a strong connection. It was clear that they were there for me and to know and feel that support lifted me so much.

The operation itself was deemed successful and at that point I thought I was over the worst. But more tests were needed. There was a suspicion that my liver might have been affected – so they wanted to be doubly sure that the cancer hadn't spread. Suffice to say, the two weeks I had to wait for the results were some of the most painful days I can remember. Thankfully I got the all clear.

During the period where I underwent tests and prior to the operation, I'd taken two weeks off work. During this time in limbo I could feel my passion for business evaporating further. Then, in a desperate bid to distract myself from morose thoughts, I picked up a business book I'd had lying around and, as I read, my thoughts were inspired again – particularly regarding my concerns with the unsettled CreaseStream project. It was like someone had switched a light back on in my head.

If You Bungle It, Own It. Then Fix It

As I considered everything more, I realised that I had it all wrong. At the genesis of the whole CreaseStream idea, I'd been aiming for an entry-level machine that could automatically feed, crease and micro-perforate digitally printed stocks at high speeds for a cost of around £4000. But what I'd actually come up with, after a long and painful discovery and testing process, was something completely different. What I had was nothing more than a Frankenstein's Monster, retailing at ten grand!

In a nutshell, in my desire to fulfil my vision, I'd

made a critical inventing error: I'd allowed the process to cloud my perspective – and the result was that CreaseStream plus was, as I had earlier suspected, over engineered. It was a humbling revelation, but the evidence had been under my nose all along. What I needed now was a compromise solution – something to sit in the market, above the base level, a £1700 hand cranked desktop machine, that wasn't prohibitively expensive to own and overly complex to operate. And I needed something fast.

It was time to re-invent...

In the months after my surgery, I'd be lying if I didn't admit that I struggled at times with my attitude and positivity. I'd get rushes of enthusiasm, followed by spells of lethargy and complete disinterest. I didn't let it get to me too much though. While the aftermath, both physical and emotional, of the illness was hampering my progress at times, the curve was an upward one on the whole. I always felt that, given time, I'd get over it.

During this unsettling period, I still managed to find time to look closely at the original design of the product. Several aspects stood out glaringly. Firstly, the feeder design seemed like it could easily be tweaked. Four belts and two feeding heads really weren't necessary – this was definitely one area where I'd over-engineered. I'd compare it to bandaging your whole leg to cover a small cut, when a simple plaster would do. The obvious thing to do was to remove some of the bells and whistles to create a much simpler auto-feed that needed just one belt and one feeding head. There were a couple of other alterations that could easily be incorporated too. As an inventor it was amazing to come to the realisation that you'd simply put too much into your creation.

During the process that led to this rather simple realisation, I think some people close to me could see that I was under pressure, and so they tried to protect me from putting myself through the stress of it all – advising that it might be better to give up and focus on some more hand feed machines that wouldn't need a feeder at all. Even Sue and I had a bit of a rare argument. She was suggesting that it was just my pride that was driving this on – that it was all becoming an unhealthy obsession. I can honestly say that it never felt that way to me.

Although it's a pretty normal and natural thing to assume, none of this had anything to do with pride. I just kept thinking we were always on the verge of a major discovery, and so I kept moving forward, pushing Paul and everyone else associated with the project, until the realisation came. To me there is a fine line between being driven by pride and believing/knowing that you have it in you to crack the code. For me it is always – with very rare exceptions – the latter. And in this case the result was the award winning CreaseStream mini range, which is now, five years down the line, a very significant part of the business.

For the record, other than during those few months after diagnosis, I have never dwelled on the fact I survived cancer. Like most things, I think I viewed it as a problem to solve, albeit that it was medicine/doctors that solved it for me. Again, during this difficult time, I learned more about myself, and in doing so used tough moments as a springboard for moving my inventing life forwards again.

"I have not failed. I've just found 10,000 ways that won't work." — Thomas A. Edison

Chapter 8

I've Done It. Now... How About You?

YOU'RE PROBABLY still wondering how on this earth a normal guy like me, who worked on a factory floor, could possibly create, market and sell an invention with enough proceeds to create a multi-million pound business!

Let me tell you this much: it wasn't easy, and for certain, without Sue standing with me none of this would have ever been possible. She had the business skills and the depth of understanding in key areas of finance and planning that were pivotal. There were many hurdles along the way and many moments where I questioned myself, based on years of conditioning, and doubted whether I actually did belong in the business circles that I now seemed to inhabit.

I guess part of me always wanted to prove something to all of those that doubted me: the mates in the pub that thought my job was stupid, the bosses that never rated me as a print finisher, or the various people along the way that thought my product would never amount to anything. Not just that, more than anything else I also wanted to prove something to myself – that I was somebody and had the wherewithal to do great things – even if I didn't have a degree from University or any certificates on my wall. To that end, overcoming the doubters, the naysayers, and Graham Harris self-sabotaging Graham Harris, has been huge and continual motivation for me. It really helps to have a driver with that kind of pulling-power.

One thing I'm very serious about communicating is the feeling you get from bringing your own invention to market from scratch. It's almost impossible to describe. The satisfaction, the pride, the excitement and euphoria you experience can be overwhelming at times – as you pass through the many obstacles in the way of finally seeing a finished product, in a box, shiny and ready for sale.

For some the process might only take a year, and for others it may take five or ten. And even then there is no guarantee of the level of success that might be reached. But if you are thinking about trying to develop your own ideas, or if you have already settled on one and got further with turning it into a prototype or a viable product, I want to encourage you to keep finding that desire to continue moving forward, despite the hurdles you face.

Inventing isn't restricted to a certain type of person either; it is open to anyone who commits to the act of believing that anything is possible. From that point of view it goes somewhat against all of that uniformity we were taught at school, where we all collectively adhered to a set of educational rules and theories. Really, regardless of our station in life, we have a blank canvas to start with if we want one. Our spare time is our own to do exactly what we like with it – without a Sir or Miss telling us to stop staring out of the window or chewing our pencil.

The open space in your mind is a blank canvas too, especially if you are doing something repetitive or mundane in your daily life right now. Just as you might sometimes use that space to dream about the perfect holiday you'd go on, you could also use it to spirit up ways of solving problems that just might lead to a product people would buy.

With that in mind, I'd like to suggest, based on

my experience, how *you* could tackle the idea of creating a product and taking it to market like I have. But while I've described how I went from the factory floor to owning not just one but two successful companies, scattering in a few helpful tips along the way, I don't profess to have all the answers. I'm not the authority, but I do know what worked for me. Hopefully some of it will resonate with whatever innovative mojo is inside you, and prompt you to get up one morning, like I did, and utter the immortal words, "I can do better than this…"

To help, I'm going to share aspects of what makes me tick – the habits, personality traits and motivations, all of which, when rolled together, have allowed me to achieve what I've achieved from these undeniably normal beginnings. And the reason for doing that is – as much as we're all fundamentally different – maybe, just maybe, you'll identify something from how I approach inventing that'll light that crucial spark in you.

Long Odds

Experts estimate that only one out of every five thousand inventions undergo successful product launches to the extent they result in a good return for their inventor. Consensus also suggests that the actual idea itself is only 10% of the process. The remainder encompasses the disciplines of manufacturing, testing, marketing and getting the product out there. While I can't verify the accuracy of these figures, from personal experience they wouldn't surprise me at all.

However, when you compare those chances with the fourteen million to one odds of winning the lottery, they actually start seeming quite attractive. Yet, people still pour a lot of passion into buying lottery tickets every week, hoping against hope, trusting to complete luck, that their numbers will come up. Admittedly I myself tried the lottery three times before I started inventing. But then, when I made the decision to embark on this inventing journey, I chose simply to trust my own ability to improve my situation. And now, having succeeded 'in the one in five thousand' lottery game, it saddens me that so many still choose to trust more to luck than their own ability to create the change in our life we all so want.

Therefore, instead of saying, "If only I could win the lottery, I would buy a new house and a new car," and dealing with the likelihood of failure fifty two weeks of the year, wouldn't it be better to try the other, inventing route that offers substantially better odds?

Furthermore, I'd like to think that if people that are *really* serious about developing ideas and making money from them read this book, those five thousand to one odds might improve dramatically.

If you are one of those people who are really serious about finding and developing the next best thing and changing your life on the back of it, then some tough love from someone who has been there and come out the other end is surely a good place to start. To that end, the starting point has to be a **sustainable desire to take action**. This is different from and much more important than just 'passion'. Obviously a bit of passion helps, but it can die a quick death when something doesn't go to plan. As Mike Tyson once famously said, "Everyone's got a plan until they're punched in the face." It's so true.

I've attended various meetings with all kinds of organisations. I've seen people present ideas with huge passion and enthusiasm: saving money, new design projects or just raising funds – it doesn't matter what the goal actually is. They say all the right things but then guess what? They want someone else to actually *do* it. "You can have that one on me. I'm too busy to carry it through," they say – while assuming that they've done enough, just by virtue of the fact that they've brought some or other genius concept to the table.

Ideas Alone Are Not Enough

This isn't to say that I'm not sometimes impressed by people's ideas. Many times I am, but more often I'm irritated by what doesn't happen afterwards, to the extent that I sometimes wish that they'd never put the idea forward at all! The sad truth is that, when the 'idea creator', for want of a better term, defers for whatever reason, someone else in the room very rarely takes these ideas forward. And even if they do, rarely do they live up to the passion with which they were initially presented. And this is how it often plays out with invention...

Too many people think that's it's just a matter of dreaming up a great idea and then passing it onto someone who they think can turn it into colossal money. I briefly felt that way about my Tri-Creaser. Some of these people start with good intentions I'm sure. But I've found that their desire ebbs away the moment they're confronted by a standard obstacle – like having to do research, find a potential manufacturer or spend some money. I always say that ideas are ten a penny. Everyone has them, but the trick is to make one stick.

In general, I think I have developed an indifference to "ideas people". Nowadays they get little respect from me unless they make it happen themselves. I'd much rather see some of these types of people own their ideas, and then try to drive them forward. But it very rarely happens that way – simply because progress takes a lot of effort and commitment to get a product off the ground.

More often I see success come from average ideas that are carried out with deep passion and commitment. The people who create such opportunities will always have my total attention and admiration. Show me a doer instead of a thinker and I'll point at something of value instead of an empty space. Show me a thinker who is *also* a doer and I'll point at someone that can change the world.

Although they can have some undeniably good ideas, lots of these types have come to me over the years to seek my advice. If their product isn't within my particular field of expertise, I'll say very little about a subject I'm not qualified to discuss. If I *can* advise and even direct them to contacts I can help with, like packaging, manufacturing or marketing, I'll sometimes do so.

But even on the occasions when I've done that, I can often hear the deflation in their voice, or see the obvious signs of resigned body language, when they realise that I'm just not going to do it for them. I can sense their passion shrinking away and I recognise that vulnerability because I've been there myself. Furthermore, I'm not the best person to advise those with ideas or inventions that they just want to licence to someone else and get out with a quick pay off. I had no choice to do it myself because I got turned down flat on several occasions.

Unfortunately, many of these people see themselves as a ready-made genius already, and usually want to piggyback on my success in some way. They want me, or someone I might recommend, to market their product or take it on and pay them royalties or some other collaboration that means they have to do less. With patents to my name and many more pending, I don't need or want to do this.

I had two visits from a plumber who came to my office with his wife to ask what I thought of this idea he had to bring a plumbing product to market. I told him that I was no expert in plumbing, but felt that he may have something. I even took him to a meeting with the engineering company we use, and did him a favour by getting him a really cheap rate for having a proto-type knocked up (and by the way, they were impressed too). I then advised him on how he should package his product and, at that moment, I could actually see him having second thoughts.

The next I heard was that he had put his idea on the back burner and got busy with his day job, putting this decent opportunity on indefinite hold. For some reason, people opt out when work needs to be done. The initial idea is so exciting, but they can't maintain that feeling. People look at me and think it must have been easy and then, when they start the process them-selves, they realise it isn't. Having an idea and taking it full circle on your own can take a monumental effort.

Sadly, for these and other reasons, many poten-tially good inventions never get past this embryonic stage. For that reason, I'm strongly suggesting that you don't become one of these rather non-committed 'ideas' people. By all means find that solution to a problem, but thereafter commit to taking the process further.

As well as ideas people who never have any inten-tion of moving their project forward, there are also a proportion of people who have equally great ideas but are seemingly in no position, in their present situation, to carry them out. I often find that these people would walk the ends of the earth to make their dreams come true but see no point in even starting. Maybe they're working long hours just to stay afloat, maybe they have a large mortgage or rent to cover. They might even be the sole earner in their family with children to feed. I completely understand how these scenarios can seem insurmountable at times.

Despite these conditions, a proportion of these people will still feel that, with enough time, they are more than capable of creating something for themselves, instead of being resigned to a long life of working for someone else. If you're one of these people, I'm here to tell you that there is a channel open to you that can change your life. There's genuine hope that can result in you realising your true potential and living the kind of life you previously thought was only available to the special few. That channel, in the first instance, isn't inventing. That part comes later. There's an important mind-set to take on board first...

The Contradiction That is Me

While identifying a common mind-set that's important to invention, it's important to acknowledge that every one of us who goes down the inventing route is different. So at this stage it's worth mentioning that there's a fundamental contradiction of personality at the heart of *my* inventor persona – and by extension it fuels my sustainable desire to take action.

On one hand I think I'm quite lazy and laid back. Honestly, if I could find a way of going about life whereby I don't need to put in the effort that walking involves, I'd probably do it. If there's a way to make a mundane daily task easier, I'm definitely behind the idea of discovering it. Honestly I'm the worst DIY candidate on earth. Sue has to really get on my case to even get me to cut the lawn. She thinks that jobs of that kind are things I should really enjoy doing and at times I've tried to see it that way.

But the truth is that tasks like DIY or lawn mowing are just *necessities* in my mind. I have no passionate attachment to them whatsoever. And there's part of me that thinks that if I'm lazy and want to do less if possible, there's a fair chance that a large proportion of my potential customers want to do less too. In a sense my lazy nature gets channelled into the creation of solutions while, in turn, the products feed upon my customers' natural affinity to think and do less. It makes perfect sense when you think about it!

But then the other side of me is that part of me that becomes driven to extremely single-minded levels when I sense that I'm onto something. I'll work night and day, days on end – never satisfied until I've achieved what I've set out to do. That's the part that pushes me through the hoops that inevitably must be navigated to make an idea a reality. When I'm in that mode it feels like I'm being swept along on the crest of a wave that never breaks. It just keeps rolling, building from peak to new peak. I'm just riding it, using muscles I never knew existed, until the objective is achieved. It's a totally exhilarating feeling and it's available to everyone.

What's Your Comfort Zone?

Obviously, at times these two character traits sit uncomfortably beside one and other. But at the same time I think they complement each other in a way that works for me. I think nothing of sitting in the office, staring into space, daydreaming about all manner of ideas.

My father-in-law thinks that I just sit in an office all day replying to the occasional email. What I do isn't physical work in his eyes and I occasionally feel a bit guilty about it – that somehow I found a way around that kind of work-your-fingers-to-the-bone life. And then he tells me how he used to work twelve-hour days, seven days a week to feed the family and the way he measures people is by the rough of their hands or the grime under their fingernails. I'll listen, because I respect him. Because I've been in the situation, I'm even more determined to drive forward, in my own way, to make sure that I never revisit my previous career world again.

In Tech-ni-Fold therefore, I have created a place where these two sides to my character can co-exist. I'm driven by the sheer love of creating things and moving the business forward. If I wasn't, I wouldn't be motivated to do any of it. I've often thought, usually during one of those office daydream moments, about problems that could potentially be solved outside of my industry. But I'm a realist too and I know full well that the reason I've never done anything about them is that the passion and motivation just isn't there. Maybe I also feel slightly uncomfortable and deterred by the fact that I don't have the same level of knowledge or experience in other areas as I possess in my own sector. But the truth is that nothing, not yet at least, has ever intrigued me sufficiently outside of the comfort zone that I operate within.

Prior to having my own company I figured that

if I was going to spend twelve hours a day in a print factory then I was at least going to try and enjoy it. Coming up with quick-fix ideas on how to improve the functionality of a print finishing machine might have seemed a little sad to some of my colleagues, but to me it was a passion, it made time go faster, and it delivered to me an alternative self-taught apprenticeship leading to the wonderful life I lead now, one where I exercise my creativity on a daily basis. I now have 71 granted patents and 10 pending – and many of these were born out of what I discovered during my time working for someone else, keeping my eyes open and going out of my way to solve problems.

A great starting point therefore would be to find that area of interest that truly gets your juices flowing, and then build everything else around that. Once you find that one thing that motivates you, only then can you even start the conversation as to whether there's a problem within that sphere that's just crying out for you to solve. And there's no doubt that the best ideas come out of an environment that is familiar to the creator. You may be a decorator, shop worker, secretary, an engineer, nurse or a fireman. Whichever it is, ask yourself probing questions about what is happening at work. Or, to be more precise, focus on what is happening very slowly or isn't happening at all. What does your day involve, where do you go, what do you see, and what might you fix?

From there, try to arrive at a simple solution that seems obvious, but at the same time might fix something, start something or end something. As a knowledgeable person in your area of work or daily environment, you should have a good idea what your solution might mean to people in your area of expertise. Then you need to be able to say to yourself: *if I could solve that problem it would make me a millionaire...*

Identify The Problem First

The majority of people's idea of a true inventor – and maybe you too have this image in your head – is a mad professor type in a white coat, working in a lab, or a slightly eccentric loner producing hundreds of crazy gadgets in his garden shed. Whatever you think, inventors seem to have this negative image of being misguided geniuses who randomly create complicated prototypes that aren't relevant in today's world, who once in a while come up with a brilliant idea only to be ripped off by a mega corporate company.

Actually, some of those descriptions, although slightly exaggerated, aren't too far away from the truth. Inventors often do hide themselves away, and don't surface until they have come up with something useful to someone. But unfortunately, too often it might only be useful to themselves. After all, it is a fact that only one invention out of every 5,000 ever makes back the money inventors paid on their patent fees.

So, forget about starting out as an inventor, tucked away in isolation. You must first go out and search for problems to solve. Think about it, everyone has been in a situation at work, in a pub, restaurant or library – out walking your dog or watching the workers mixing cement on the street – where we've looked at something that's being done and thought, "Surely there's a quicker way of doing *that*?"

In that situation the word quicker can easily be interchanged with easier, cheaper or just simply 'better'. Regardless, when you come across one of these moments, that is the time to not assume that it's someone else's problem to come up with the new way, but instead to take on that responsibility yourself. And when you make just that small decision, when you give in to that tiny shift in responsibility, although you can't call yourself an inventor quite yet, you're at least knocking on the door that leads to the world of invention.

So before opening that door, it's important to choose something you are (a) passionate about and (b) in an area that you are familiar with. I chose my own world of print finishing – where my colleagues routinely invented makeshift solutions that might have consisted of sticky tape and cardboard – to achieve a temporary solution to whatever problem that occurred during production. But these ideas came and went, with nobody really stopping to think about their viability for very long.

Granted, many of these spur-of the-moment solutions wouldn't have been saleable. But at the same time, I have also seen a fair few hashed-up assemblies that, with a bit of thought and application, could have become actual products. All it needed was a bit of imagination – like envisaging a house that you want to buy, with no carpets and peeling paint, with your furniture in it. An important part of inventing is the ability to look beyond the cardboard and the sticky tape towards something that's created in the same shape and image – only more evolved and packed in a nice box ready to sell to the waiting masses. That end point is when you can call yourself an inventor, but there are a few steps that should come first.

Be Clear About Your Goal

At the core of my 'inventor mind' is the idea that I need to be absolutely positive that whatever I am trying to improve, a process or application for example, is needed to the extent that people would be willing to pay a premium to get it. Otherwise I'd be spending my time fixing someone's problem only to end up broke in the end.

Beware though, many inventors, whether they'd admit it or not, get into inventing as a means of creating something that makes them look clever, but that people may not ultimately need. Often the simplest ideas are the best and, after all, nobody really wants something that is overly complex to use. So try and keep it simple where possible. That would be the starting point as opposed to picking an overly complicated idea.

The need to make money sounds like the wrong footing from which to start a project, but really it is the only sensible way to approach it. The truth is, genuinely successful inventors that are willing to push through the barriers at each stage of the process, often end up running businesses and paying patent fees, wages and bargaining for yet more patent applications. It is an undeniably expensive cycle. This doesn't mean to say that I don't get passionate and motivated about improving my customers working lives when I'm coming up with a new idea; that's a huge part of the force that drives me too. But the concept of improving lives can be the be-all and end-all. Everyone has to make a living and improve his or her own situation at the same time.

And there's one more element – and I think it rings true with a vast proportion of inventors that I've run into over the years – whereby I always feel a need to justify myself in terms of my value to the world. When I consider *why* I think this way, it usually comes down to the fact that I feel, rightly or wrongly, that I may not have reached what others might consider to be my potential in certain areas – or at least may not have conformed to certain familiar conventions. That's just my personal take on it. And my response to that is to reach potential in other ways, my *own* ways.

So, one of the messages in this book that I'd like to be crystal clear is that anyone, no matter how well they did at school, whether they have a degree or certification in some field or not, can become a successful inventor that earns a good living. I'm *convinced* that potential is in everyone, but the route to that point will inevitably be different in every case. The best I can do is explain how I approach this lifestyle, in the hope that people can extract something from what I say and apply it to their particular idea or set of circumstances.

Don't Assume That Somebody Has Already Tried

Part of creating a valuable solution is in not assuming that someone previously tried to solve the problem and failed. As strange as it may sound, sometimes a solution is so simple that anyone that's immersed in the industry is just too close to it and conditioned by the inherent issues to be able to step back and see what's potentially right in front of them. Granted, in many cases there are good reasons why a particular problem won't go away. Remember, when I was first pitching the idea of the Tri-Creaser, several big company representatives said to me often, "If it could be done, we'd have done it by now." They were wrong in that assumption, but occasionally it is true.

Even so, an important facet of the inventing discipline – in addition to helping your customers and maintaining your reputation – is the belief that, as hard as it may seem and as much perseverance is required – there is always a way to, at the very least, improve something that's already out there. A complete solution just may not be possible.

I've often thought that cat's eyes are one of the great inventions of all time. In 1933 Percy Shaw was caught up in fog whilst driving and the only light he could see was a red glare from a cat he'd spotted by the side of the road, seemingly being reflected back at him by his car headlights. Percy had the forethought to react to what he saw and to recreate that glare in the middle of the road with glass, so that our car headlights would reflect back at us.

The idea of cat's eyes might seem simple at first look, but apparently there is a lot more to them than you may be aware of. They are designed to self-clean by way of a combination of soaked up rainwater and from cars driving over them. I bet Percy thought, "Surely nobody has tried this?" In those days he was possibly right.

But nowadays, with technology moving very fast, many people assume that someone has already tried all the best ideas. Martin Dick didn't think that. In 1990 he came up with an idea to improve the efficiency of the cat's eye by producing a Solarite road-stud that gave out ten times more reflection. Just like Percy, he became a wealthy man. Look in your environment for what may not exist. But also consider what might benefit from improvement.

The First Steps To Making It Happen...

My first invention was special in the sense that it was a valuable solution to an industry-wide problem. I often ask myself how that happened – why I was able to hit the bull's-eye with my first dart? After all, many of my other inventions have been less ground-breaking on paper, but nevertheless, very profitable in their own right in the sense that they form part of our product range and give our customers ready packaged solutions in other areas of print finishing. I'm in no doubt that I was fortunate to be able to finance all my other ideas because of the success of the first, but I could have done it the other way around.

So the message there is that it isn't necessary to find that one-off, golden solution that will transform your life with your first idea. That just happened to be how it worked for me. Instead, focus on something that's realistic and achievable with the time, money and expertise that you have. Start with the cardboard and sticky tape version if you have to – and then move it forward step-by-step from there.

Do Your Homework...

When I say do your homework, I mean *really* carry out some serious research. Don't play at it, or cut corners. There's a possibility that some versions of your idea are out there already, but you may have something that improves on all of them and has better functionality – which can often mean that it is patentable (more of that later). So many first time inventors have a romantic notion that they can think up a fabulous idea first time, yet they give up the ghost if they get even the slightest

190

hint that something similar is out there. Rather than feeling deflated, take a continually optimistic approach and study the competition. You might even be able to design around what someone else has; that happens all the time. But if you hit a dead end, don't bale out. Just think up another problem to solve. Keep focused and, above all else, be persistent.

In my case, when I created a rotary retrofit solution to micro-perforate paper, I studied the existing methods and found out that one of the reasons why there wasn't a better product out there was that the manufacturers relied on their perforation blades to wear out and break so their customers bought more. It was planned obsolescence if you like – and this consumable aspect was making them a lot of money. We, the industry, just shrugged and accepted it.

When I studied *why* the blades were breaking it was pretty obvious: they were made of thin steel that rusted virtually overnight. Not just that, they were running against a steel anvil below that combined to produce a scissor action into the sheet. Predictably, as time went on, the punctures made in the paper stock became rougher and rougher – to the extent that it was a bit like trying to cut your nails with blunt scissors or shaving with a worn razor blade. The teeth on the blade would often break off and for £10 we could replace it from the stock held at the supplier every time we ran a job. Blade after blade would rust and wear out, and print companies spent hundreds of pounds every year replacing them. But that's just how it was.

When I visited my customers, of course many of them complained about these rough results. But all of them assumed that, if it could be improved, then surely manufacturers would have done it by now. How wrong could they be? Instead, they just found ways around it to keep jobs moving. I knew my customers would simply perforate offline and would then feed the sheets through their machines to be folded. They weren't shy about telling me this either. Outsourcing to a platen (flat platform) cylinder – a primitive machine designed for just that one purpose – was of course expensive, but the results were undeniably very good. The downside however was the delay caused by moving the job to the business with a platen cylinder and waiting for it to come back.

Consequently, my thinking involved looking at the process and the result achieved by the platen cylinder. And when I did, in my head it seemed simple: I needed to replicate its capabilities for my own purposes. A very fine perf-blade would contact the sheet, not in a scissor action, but instead by making contact with a hard steel blanket in a striking motion. The blade would just penetrate the sheet and stop short of pushing coarsely through it.

By studying the processes, I'd identified the problem and also what I saw as the solution and my first task was to replicate those fine perforation blades and it took me six months to find a supplier, who I then asked to strengthen the blade and make it out of their strongest steel. I was adamant that I didn't want my blade to retro-fit the existing holding collar that held those rusty throw away blades, so I changed the inner dimension and got my engineering company to produce my own (holding collar).

Then I found a plastic supplier and asked them to produce some circular anvils to run my blade on – this step took two months to perfect because I had to achieve precisely the right dimensions for the blade to meet. All of this wasn't so much super-inventive as just plain logical. Obviously it took some engineering excellence and advice from those guys to help me achieve the desired results, using the best quality/most appropriate materials. But it was the combination of that backup and my logical approach that meant that the inventing process came together very nicely.

Go Again, And Again...

For someone new to inventing, I totally recognise that this all sounds very difficult. You're on your own; it might feel like you're a long way from a product and just fitting random shapes together. You might feel like giving up but *this* is when you dig in and persevere. And then you go again the next day and the next day until you turn a corner and a miracle happens. If you believe it enough and work hard, it will.

Look at it this way: if a hitch arises along the way, know that you've got this far. Surely you're not going to leave it there and let a lot of hard work go to waste? Go the other way. Become *obsessed* about solving the problem but in a very meticulous, logical way. I've found that just telling yourself that you can solve a solution to one of the big problems in your environment is a great motivator. It is exciting, exhilarating and fulfilling, and if you grind it out and put in the hours you will find it rewarding.

And remember: it hasn't always come easy to me. In fact, it is not unusual for me to be staring at some prototype I have been testing for hours, just a series of shapes like you might have in front of you now, thinking to myself: *What if I tried this silly thing, or turned things upside down?*

Furthermore, from experience, sometimes it's during these reflective moments where you're open to anything, willing to go down any avenue with no fear of judgement, when eureka moments happen. So my advice would be to embrace that time, even seek it out – as I do in a way now with my staring-into-space moments at my desk. All too often I've found that individuals, at some relaxed seminar or workshop when there's no pressure to come up with anything, conceive fantastic creations and thought processes. But that same person clams up when they use their or their own company's time. They hear the clock ticking and any creative headspace dissolves. It is like me answering a question on a TV quiz. Once the clock ticks out loud my mind goes blank. I need to work in a relaxed environment; problem solving lends itself to this.

Many people don't get past this crucial prototype stage either. Sometimes they meet with a potential investor and get frustrated when they get rejected. They even blame the investor and develop a bitterness and arrogance that is off-putting to everybody. I met a clever guy at a trade show once, six or seven years ago. He showed me two wonderful products that he'd developed; he had patents in place. Then he told me that he'd had rejections from major companies and it took me not very long to figure out why. He was wearing worn out jeans and a T-shirt – which he accompanied with an arrogant swagger, while he told everyone who'd listen that the people who'd turned him down were idiots because they wouldn't listen to his demands.

These types of inventors don't realise that *they* are the ones being rejected, not their products – because the truth is, manufacturers don't have the time or energy to work with people with attitude. I gave this guy some tough love in the form of some observations based on what I'd experienced, and he didn't take any of it on board. There's nothing as sad as watching an inventor getting in the way of a good deal. And he's still working his day job…

Don't Seek Feedback Or Advice From Family Or Friends

Warning: This might seem a little contentious, but I truly believe that those closest to a would-be inventor can either falsely build up their hopes or talk them out of a good idea altogether. New inventors can feel vulnerable and isolated in their quest to create something unique. And the temptation to seek positive feedback and acceptance, and in some cases, adulation, can be overwhelming. Don't do it!

Most successful inventors are often told how crazy their ideas are during the planning stage yet their products hit the market and wow us all. Imagine if those types of people had listened to their friends or a family member and been put off. I honestly believe that if someone puts in the research and studies the market opportunity for their invention, then they shouldn't desire the opinion of someone who doesn't have the benefit of that insight.

Yes, there will be times when some inventors need to disclose information to their nearest and dearest – for instance if they seek financial backing from them or if their idea is impacting on a spouse's time or resources, but on the whole I would advise against it. If you've really done your research and homework, you shouldn't need someone else's reassurance anyway. Keep it to yourself!

The Proof Of The Pudding Really Is In The Eating

When it came to testing my work, I was pretty confident based on the logic that I had applied along the way. Yes it was laborious and time consuming at times, but the attention to detail meant that I'd eliminated many of the potential failings as I went along. And the initial results bore that out. They were incredible. The great quality engineering, stronger, tougher blades and a few obvious tweaks soon became that product that could be packed in a nice box, complete with an easy to understand instruction leaflet.

Obviously problems crop up once a product is on the market. In this case some of my customers complained about high or low perforation points on the sheet. The problem lay with the blades themselves so I sent them back and found another supplier. It was a problem I had to fix and that lesson is one of the many facets of being an inventor: something will always go wrong (and it's part of the process to find a solution).

Failure Is One Of The Keys To Success

Recently I came up with an invention idea. It was awful. Here's why...

I encountered a problem while I was out walking my dog. I took an umbrella with me because it was pouring down with rain, but I still ended up getting soaked. It happened because my dog crouched down to do what dogs do, and I couldn't deal with scooping the mess with my bag without having three pairs of hands. And then the umbrella flew off, leaving me exposed to the deluge. "Aha, is this a problem for most dog walkers?" I thought.

For a short time I had fun trying to solve this problem because it had happened to me before. I relished thinking about some ideas – such as having a sharp point at the base of the umbrella handle so I could stab it in the field next to the dog poop as I bent down to tend to it. However it didn't take me long to realise that there wasn't a problem to solve other than one that was unique to Graham Harris, not the population at large. The solution was simple: wear a raincoat with a hood. That was the end of that idea.

What I'm getting at is that part of the challenge of invention and the problem solving process that goes hand in hand with it, is knowing that every failure or dead-end idea is an important and essential step to finding the solution you are seeking. It might sound crazy, but finding out what doesn't work is a very good thing. By making mistakes, really you've narrowed down your options and you're one step closer to knowing what *does* work. This information is vital for any inventor, so you should also document the steps you take along the way, successful or otherwise. You'll be amazed how often you'll come back to a note or a comment, possibly for something completely unrelated.

Here's an example. Eventually I used rubber O-rings to crease paper. But they weren't my first choice as a potential solution to the problem of cracking printed stock – far from it. I used everything I could think of prior to that – including plastic and soft copper. At the start, I hazarded a guess that both would be preferable to using steel, which just seemed to rip the sheets in half. But I soon found out that these were just as harsh, and once I did, I never went there again.

Before I gave up on them though, I changed their dimensions and had them made in all kinds of shapes and profiles. Annoyingly, although there was some improvement, it was never going to be good enough. They were all still too destructive. So I rejected the materials I had used but still carried over those shapes and profiles to create in some other material. Although I'd failed in the attempt or at least hit a glitch, I still carried knowledge forward from doing so. So, throw as many darts as possible at the board and see what sticks in.

All the time I was thinking on multiple levels as to how to maximise the eventual saleability of my newfound solution. I was better placed than most to understand the inner thoughts of print finishers; I knew they would be put-off by laboured hit-and-miss setting procedures. Instead they needed something simple to replace their conventional devices. If I was going to develop something special I wasn't going to settle for something that the next guy could design around and beat.

In the background, I had also created some shapes for the channels below where the creasing profile ran into. When I eventually arrived at using rubber as my base material, those profiles and shapes helped considerably. With rubber I used its flexibility not only to create a soft and gentle crease in the paper, but I also used it to find a way to achieve quick setting choices for the operators using my device. Rolling an O-ring into several positions to achieve instant depths and crease strengths to get the desired results in any situation, definitely trumped the slow engagement, disengagement of the original scoring products rigid steel discs.

Meanwhile I covered lots of ground by testing more ideas and pushing something good into something special. Part of developing a product is in making it look great. For example, adding colour coding to help the operator get to the setting faster helped its perceived value. We put splashes of paint on the rubber and corresponding dots of paint on the opposing channels – small improvements that made all the difference.

But there is a cut off point, you need to stop the tinkering and get to market and start selling. You can start to develop the improved version when your customers tell you what is lacking. You can start to design it in your time between sales calls and nail it when you have thought it through and found time. Listen to more customers, they will have more comments, write them down and collate them, ponder over them for a while but don't lose focus on the existing product that is bringing food to your table, the time will come for the next version, your customers are just happy for now that you made their life easier. The next steps will follow.

It might even be that you need to give up on what you have created completely and start again with something that has more market potential, or is cheaper to nurture. Whatever you do, don't let pride and the eagerness to prove others wrong be your sole motivation to keep hold of an idea you know is draining your resources and cash. The smarter thing to do is to cut your losses and start again—this is what successful inventors have to do at times. Look at it not like the end of the road, but more like the start of a new one.

Become The Three-year Old Version Of You

Finally, and this is a belief that still rings true with me, one of the best traits an inventor can have is to retain a childlike inquisitiveness and ask those so-called "crazy" questions that people are too embarrassed to ask – like when a child says to his grandparent, "Grandad, why don't you have any hair?" Everyone just stares, but it's a fair question.

Secretly we all admire those people because these are the questions we all wish we had the courage to air. My advice would always be to risk being thought of as stupid because trust me that will be temporary. You wouldn't believe how many inventions have come about as a result of something so simple, so 'stupid' – simply borne out of child-like curiosity. Unfortunately, most people don't want to be the one who gets laughed at because of a crazy idea or suggestion. People hate rejection and nods of disapproval, so they come up with something safe and sensible as a result. The problem is: safe and sensible ideas don't get patented and they don't change lives – yours or anyone else's.

Beyond that, the act of being inquisitive can present as a form of "mind ping-pong" in solitude. Coming up with obscure ideas to find a solution to a problem by batting ideas to your imaginative subconscious and seeing what comes back can be very positive. At the very least you are challenging yourself by pushing the boundaries of logic and of possibility. After all, history is littered with examples of great ideas that have appeared out of nowhere, where the inventor, pushing for something else, stumbles upon an idea or invention that can change the world. Penicillin and *Scotchguard* are two great examples.

In the first instance, Alexander Fleming stumbled upon his invention when he noticed a growth of mould in a petri dish that had been left close to an open window. He then discovered, by chance, that the bacteria that had formed around the mould were the key. From there Penicillin was developed. None of it was planned; it just happened in the course of the process of looking for solutions.

Similarly, Patsy Sherman, a chemist hired to research rubber linings for aircraft fuel lines in the early 1950s, dropped a bottle of synthetic latex she'd made on the floor, splashing her assistant's shoes in the process. To their surprise they found that the substance didn't alter the appearance of the shoes, but, critically, it appeared to repel water, oil and other fluids. By pure accident, they had discovered stain and water repellent that could be applied to all manner of items.

If these two events can happen and change the world, many more can too. Although this type of thing hasn't quite happened to me in the same way, I have forced "accidents" to happen in order to get the actual result I set out to achieve – usually in a completely different way than I could have initially imagined. I've had such events happen to me, usually late at night when I've exhausted all the ideas I'd planned to try. I could be sitting with a pile of components and I might decide simply to randomly deconstruct them in a disorderly and obscure manner, then reconstruct them introducing old parts I previously used or even rejected from another project. Then, when I look at their new formation and test the results, I might find I have achieved something amazing – and have to then work out how on earth it all happened.

It might sound careless, desperate, or even a bit foolish, but you've got to be in this frame of mind, of being open to trying anything, if you're going to invent.

Chapter 9

I.P And Protecting Your Work

DON'T people just love shortcuts?

My advice would be to not take any – particularly when it comes to protecting your ideas. I've referenced patenting a few times already and, as an inventor who has many patents, it's impossible to stress the importance of patenting your work – or your *intellectual property* to use industry terminology. Make a mistake at this stage and the idea – and all the hard work involved with development and manufacturing – is potentially wasted if the concept isn't adequately protected. You could be doing all that work for someone else to benefit.

To that end, the cost associated with patenting should be 'front and centre' in any invention's budget. But prior to that, you must establish the potential demand for the item in the first place. In my industry, before I even consider developing a solution to an unsolved problem in the print business, I have to know for sure, without any doubt whatsoever, that thousands of global print companies will buy it if it were available.

Sometimes I'm not even certain how I'll develop this idea; I just know that, if the demand is there, I'll find a way. Once I am convinced that the market is there, I then scrutinise the end result and quality that the demand market would expect from my solution. I talk to some of them and get them involved in the discussion because I know that when the product exists, they will be my first customers.

Unfortunately, many new inventors don't look at the actual demand. Instead they focus on some *per-*

*ceived le*vel of demand that's in their head based on a degree of personal experience – guesswork basically. So, before deciding to patent something you've created, you will need to know there is a demand for your invention. From this perspective I would advise that you keep things simple the first time around, so that you can focus on every aspect of getting your idea patented and eventually sold. Here are some simple steps...

What You Can Patent

A patent can be granted on something that is new, that can be made or used. The item must be inventive in terms of it being an improvement on something that already exists. To that end, you can use a patent to protect your invention. Having a patent gives you the right to take legal action against anyone who makes, uses, sells or imports it without your permission. I would advise anyone who decides to enter the patenting process to take it as seriously as starting a business or taking out a mortgage. It is not something you should go into half-heartedly. Unless you've got cash to burn, this isn't the time or place to go chasing vague, poorly researched hunches.

With that in mind, entering the patent process should really be your first building block in creating an invention driven business. Most people assume that the high incidences of launch failure are due to poor products. That's not entirely the case. More products fail because of marketing shortcomings or cash flow calamities. Because of the costs of important parts of the business like patenting, many businesses run out of money before they're even off the ground. That's a tragedy that can easily be avoided if you go into the whole exercise with a very methodical business mind. After all, if you're smart enough to come up with a good product, you're certainly smart enough to put the foundations of a sound business in place too. You must make that transition from lone inventor to business owner smoothly.

When I entered the invention world back in 1998/99, I knew that I had a year to try and sell some of my products otherwise I wouldn't be able to afford to take out international patents to protect them. The clock was ticking and I needed to react. The benefits to working through the early part of the patenting process are that you get to know the pros and cons of your invention intimately. Then, when the time comes to shout those benefits from your rooftop, get them down on paper and build something tangible to support what you have created. That might involve sending messages via social media channels, building a small website, starting a blog, knocking on doors or making phone calls – or a combination of all of these.

The day before my patent pending status was issued, I searched for the contact details of all the manufacturers who might conceivably want to produce my first product. Within only days, I was out knocking on doors to offer free demos and then called the media for free publicity. It was day-to-day hustle, and I had no qualification for any of it. But these are business traits you need to adopt to become successful. Staying in your inventor bubble won't be enough if you want to monetize.

Brace yourself though. Just like taking out a mortgage, your decision to navigate the patent process will cost you a significant amount of money – especially if you do it professionally by using a patent attorney. Fees start anywhere from £3,000 up to £6,000 in the initial U.K. filing stage, and £1,000's more if you take up the PCT (international) option after 12 months (whereby you choose specific countries where you want your patent to have effect). In fact, you could easily end up paying more in patent fees than the average mortgage repayment, but this cost should be manageable as long as you are clawing back enough profit from your invention to cover them.

As soon as I had officially filed for my first patent, I started selling my prototypes and first production devices, long before I received my patent attorney's invoice. And by the time I needed to choose the countries I would extend my patent application into, I had already sold 200 of my Tri-Creasers. I had made more than enough money to cover the patenting cost. Just like anything, I know that some inventors file their own patents, cutting out the patent Attorney or Agent, and doing it this way can be substantially cheaper. However, in my case, I didn't feel confident enough to carry this through, and the possibility of leaving a loophole for someone to exploit was a huge concern for me. Instead I decided to focus on finding professionals to help me make the patent water-tight, while I focused on getting some products out into the market

As soon as I received my patent pending status for my Tri-Creaser I used every spare hour after my daytime shift finished to travel as far as I could to show people this thing that would make their life so much easier.

To be granted a patent, your invention must be all of the following:

• Something that can be made or used

- new
- inventive - not just an obvious modification to something that already exists
- Patents are expensive and difficult to get. Before you apply, make sure the patent is right for your business because there are certain things that can't be protected.

What You Can't Patent

- Literary, dramatic, musical or artistic works
- A way of doing business, playing a game or thinking
- A method of medical treatment or diagnosis
- A discovery, scientific theory or mathematical method
- New types of plants, seeds or animals
- The way information is presented
- Some computer programs

Before You Do Anything

Patents are the most difficult form of protection to get. Check if a patent is right for your business before you apply for one.

You should only apply for a patent if:

- Your invention is new - check for similar ones by searching existing patents and products on the internet and trade publications
- You have the time and money for the application process

I put absolutely everything into my patent applications. I invite my patent Attorney over to our showroom to see the product in action – to see it working in the environment it will be available in. I usually have Paul on hand too to cover some of the technical areas I might have missed. We look at the whole process and discuss what materials we used to make the product work – as well as identifying what materials also worked well enough to include in the document. We look at shapes and sizes and all the different ways of getting the desired result, many of which I would have tried at some point along the way. **They all go in the patent.** And the reason for that is to limit the chances of a company or person 'designing around' my invention, or using a method I tried but didn't include in the patent application. Every base must be covered. Some of our patents even cover a multitude of areas that I have not yet tapped into, but might do sometime in the future.

Naturally this exhaustive process costs a lot in terms of time and money, but much more importantly it increases the chances of avoiding infringement later down the line. I spend at least two hours reading the application (patent language is different to the language we are used to) draft and amending or adding information – I cannot express how important it is to put a significant amount of time and effort into this stage. Patent attorneys need to know what it is you are trying to do, they need to know your market and the potential for your invention; it all goes in your patent application.

I have stopped at least seven infringers from exploiting my inventions so far and a lot is owed to the time I spent with my patent attorney working on tightening up my patent application.

The Application Process Is:

• **Complicated** - only 1 in 20 applicants get a patent without professional help

I know that some inventors are more than capable of doing all the work themselves, but I think that many attempt to do it just to save money, and I fear they can lose the chance of fighting off the copycats because of something they missed, or didn't do correctly. I would advise inventors to think twice about applying for a patent without professional help

• **Expensive** - with professional help, applications typically cost £4,000

• **Long** - it usually takes 5 years

Yes, it can take 5 years to receive a full patent but that doesn't mean to say that you can't begin selling your product as soon as you filed your patent application. It means you just can't sue anyone until you have full patent status, however, you can put people on notice by speaking with a lawyer and sending a letter through them – this means that for every product they sell you can receive some financial reimbursement if they lose a future case, or if you settle through litigation. If you get a patent, you'll also have to pay to renew it each year and the costs of legal action if you need to defend it.

You need to be aware that patent renewal fees are all relative. If you keep selling and making profit they shouldn't be a problem. We pay out tens of thousands of pounds each year and when that thick pile of invoices reaches my table I have to rise above the negative thoughts I have when I go through each one. I have to remind myself that without these patents we wouldn't have the business we enjoy.

In my experience it isn't the ethical corporate organisations that try to copy. Many of them don't like to be seen caught up in litigation cases; they want to play fair. In November 2011 my company, Tech-ni-Fold, managed to stop U.S. based Update Ltd and D & R Bindery from continuing to manufacture a device called the "Ultimate Score". We paid over £120,000 to protect our patents over an eighteen-month legal battle. Then, in August 2014, Tech-ni-Fold Ltd filed a lawsuit against U.S. based Rosback and we lost the case as I described earlier.

Regardless, the point is, if you truly have a great product that solves big problems for a lot of people and makes or saves them a significant amount of money, you might experience potential or actual infringement. So you need to make sure you are making enough profit per sale, so that you can put some away for that day where you might need to fight the copycats.

Other Ways To Protect Your Intellectual Property

Remember, other methods might be more appropriate for your business. For example, you can use:

• Trademarks - if you can create a brand and be first to market

• Design rights - if how your product looks (rather than how it works) is important and innovative

• Non-disclosure agreements – to keep it secret before launch. This can provide enough protection if your product is likely to sell for only a short time

I have gone into meetings with the view to collaborate with a partner in certain fields armed only with my patent. In the last few years I have insisted that companies I aim to collaborate with sign a non-disclosure, simply because there's always the possibility that they might end up not wanting your patented solution, but might nevertheless use some other unpatented ideas you brought to the table instead.

If You Decide To Apply

When you've checked that a patent is what you need, you should find a patent attorney or, at the very least, an advisor. They will:

• Help you prepare your application correctly - you can't add in additional information later

• Give you the best chance of being granted a patent

• Try to make sure that your patent is as commercially valuable as possible

Along the way, companies offering to promote your invention for a fee may approach you. Get independent legal or financial advice before you agree to anything. While it is indeed flattering to be told that your invention sounds wonderful, you should be aware that there are many companies who have impressive websites that prey on people who struggle to know what to do to promote their product. I would advise that all new inventors try to avoid these people – and instead focus on how they can build up their own confidence in what they created first. Practice a pitch and create a sell sheet or brochure that explains the benefits to the people you want to reach. Learn how to be professional and get out there.

One of the most frustrating areas of the patent process for me is paying for a search examination in order to speed things up. Designated examiners give a pre-determined amount of time to come up with patent applications that might fit into the same category as your invention and may therefore have similar claims. I used to falsely think that that was it: once the examiners had carried out their searches and found little in the way of threats, you were good to go. But it is only when you get to the litigation process, where I've been, that you realise that opposing attorneys will do their own searches and spend days digging up other patent applications with the hope that they might put up a good case as to why their client developed their product, or even render your patent invalid.

Although this method has so far proved ineffective, in my own experience it concerns me that I have already paid for search examinations. The rules are stacked against inventors in this case; they are paying costs at both ends. I also agree with James Dyson, inventor of the bag-less vacuum machine's sentiments written here:

"The Government must act to simplify the system. Patents are expensive to file in the first place. Then you've got renewal fees – there's no other walk of life where you lose your rights on your work of art if you fail to 'renew' it. And then the costs of actually fighting a case are out of this world."

He added that it could easily cost £3m to fight a case in the U.K., and "tens of millions of dollars" in the U.S. "It gets to the point where [a small business] can't afford to carry on. He also said that rights holders win only eighteen per cent of U.K. legal disputes: "The system does not support design and patent holders. You don't bring a case because of the expense and the risk that if you lose, you pay the other side's costs. The eighty-two per cent [that lose legal disputes] have gone to all the trouble and expense of developing the technology and then some company comes along and rides on their coat tails. It's grossly unfair."

Sir James suggested elements of the "simpler" German and French patent systems could be adopted in the U.K. to reduce the length, cost and complexity of cases.

Impostors

As an inventor, I stand for honesty and integrity. I also stand for justice and this is why I don't hesitate to protect my intellectual property. Believe me, there is no better feeling than to hear that someone loves what you created and then buys your solution to a problem they encounter. It is humbling to receive letters of thanks, emails and telephone calls that tell us how we made people's lives better or how we saved them money. Equally, there is no worse feeling than seeing a product that looks like ours on a rival website. And it doesn't sit well with me when I see that their marketing messages are very similar or even the same as ours. If I was to ignore it, all our livelihoods could be at risk. My team and I have worked so hard to build up our reputation and I feel I have a duty to protect them too.

At one trade show we exhibited at, one of our distributors complimented me on getting my product in another booth on a nice piece of kit. Of course I hadn't even heard of the company concerned and I certainly hadn't sanctioned this installation. I soon found myself at the booth in question, trying to prise it off the machine. The company manager told me he purchased it from one of our resellers but to me it looked inferior to one of ours. His boss then came over and tried to remove me from the stand, before admitting that they were lying – instead conceding that they had indeed manufactured it themselves. Everything calmed down and for some strange reason I found myself feeling bad. My feelings made no sense!

Then I started posing myself questions: *Did this really matter in the grand scheme of things? Should I have reacted this way?* After all, over the years I have walked by several booths that have been exhibiting copies of my Tri-Creaser or another of my products without flying off the handle and wrestling the equipment from its temporary host. Mostly I have kept calm, walked past nonchalantly, or maybe just picked up a business card to pass on to my lawyer later. But on that day, for some reason it got to me, and I reacted instinctively. Then, on the inside, I found myself backtracking. Being exploited for monetary gain can have that effect on you. I haven't reacted in such an extreme manner since.

Impostors and imitators are everywhere, sadly – particularly in the world of inventing. These are the people who, rather than take the hard road less travelled, would prefer to take the path of least resistance, which usually involves copying some or all of someone else's idea. So, I have always taken a hard line approach against companies that I believe bring out products that potentially infringe something I've worked so hard to bring to market. And can you blame me? After all, we built up a business, a life, based on a unique idea that nobody in the history of print had ever come up with. Yet, in a period of sixteen years there have been several products that have hit the market, all claiming to solve the same problem as my original Tri-Creaser.

Consequently, I have, with the help of lawyers, managed to stop five out of those six companies from continuing with their product. That should tell you how serious I am about protecting something I worked so hard to produce – and I also hope it shows my staff and all our distributors the lengths I will go to protect their livelihoods too.

From that perspective I look back at one of the biggest moments of my business life with a wry smile – that first meeting with Heidelberg after a year of rejections. As it turned out, a person sitting in those meetings soon left the German organisation to set up his own company. And as we won that amazing contract to supply Heidelberg with the initial order of 500 Tri-Creaser's, we heard that this guy was knocking out a version of our device! That was the first time I really felt that sense of running through the chambers.

Thankfully, we caught up with him – and our lawyer's letter did the trick in terms of putting paid to his shenanigans. He called to apologise, but I found out he had still sold over a hundred of his copy creasing system. The shear audacity of it amazed me. How could this have happened on the back of my very first confidential meeting with a company of Heidelberg's magnitude? What's even worse is that my German distributor told me recently that this guy admitted to him that he is just waiting for our patent to expire in a few years time so that he can jump straight back in the game again.

As stressful as all of this information is, at the heart of it is a very important realisation – one that any inventor should strive to attain. Following that Heidelberg meeting it dawned on me that I had created the kind of product that would actually *attract* this kind of situation. Tri-Creaser was really that good. People were going to want to try to copy it. I took this as a huge compliment, but it also woke me up to the fact that, if I was going to survive (and stay sane), I'd need to take appropriate action going forward.

Sue and I discussed this predicament and decided firstly to increase our selling price to compensate. In addition, we opted to create an account in which to build up finances that would service eventualities of this kind. If we needed to take legal action in the future, at least we'd be in a position to act swiftly.

Within a year of doing business we were facing another company who were selling a "copycat" system – this time on our doorstep in England. We even had to put up with taunting and abuse from this person, and a band of his followers, at a trade show. From memory, when I got a bit irate with the guy who'd made the copy, he asked me to go easy on him because he'd just had a heart bypass operation! It was surreal, and because he was a bit of a charmer, I found myself feeling a little sorry for him. But not so sorry that he didn't get a lawyer's letter within a few days, requesting that he stop.

It never ceases to amaze me how some people act in circumstances like this. I used to feel really sad at this type of behaviour. I used to wonder why people who wanted to get into a market needed to aggressively disrespect those that had opened the gate and paved the way. Furthermore, I have always said that if someone came out with an innovative product that got *around* the claims in my patent, of course I wouldn't like it, but I would definitely accept it. That's part of the skill in being an inventor: recognising what exists, and seeing if it can be improved. And if there are gaps in patents that facilitate that, then so be it. I have never ever been so naïve as to think that my first patent would be good enough to stand up alone and protect us against any competition for a full twenty years. That's a completely unrealistic position for any inventor to be in.

If anything I think of my first invention as something that other people might want to improve on or even to render it inconsequential. I've even felt that way about it myself – often thinking, "How can I improve the technology, so that when someone cracks the code of my first idea I have something much better, that raises the bar?"

When the Rosback case came about, this feeling came back to me in a way that made me think of a five-chamber 'game' where I'm working in the fifth, and they'd, by chance, just found the door that opened the first. When I looked at it in that way, it made the loss easier to take. In addition, this is why I take out new patents to protect better, more advanced technology – and this is why I spend hours every month studying the market and finding out what new problems are occurring in paper manufacturing and print processing. I do it all in a constant quest to stay ahead of our competition.

As it stands we hold 81 patents (10 are patent pending) covering the areas in our field of expertise and we have pushed that bar significantly higher over the last 10 years through our evolution. The influx of poorly made paper and recycled materials, together with amazingly difficult print applications play into our hands in that what we started off with in chamber one won't hold up to today's challenges. Chamber after chamber could possibly open up for us, so that by the time chamber five is breached by a competitor, I hope to be in chamber eight or nine. It is instilled in me that as a true innovator and market leader, I need to be at least three steps ahead of those who even begin to enter the chase.

Another motivating factor is that, as an inventor that takes my creations very seriously, I'll be the first to admit that I can be sensitive to outside threats. My upbringing and some of the rejections and adversities I've faced mean that I probably personalise things more than I should. But in my case it helps me to keep moving. And I'm always moving, thinking. When I discover something new, I won't always rush to take out a patent though, simply because the existing one might be doing its job just fine. Timing is important, and when the timing is right, only then will I meet with my patent attorney.

Amazingly, our very first patent covers only one per cent of products that we sell now. That's why the Rosback case loss was more symbolic than physically damaging. On reflection, it was the loss of the case when I felt certain of a win that grated most. The technology concerned in the case was a major breakthrough in our industry in 1999 and we made use of it for a few years until we developed a better solution. Some of our very first customers became frustrated when we presented our second phase creasing solution, covered by another patent, because it produced better results and worked well on digitally printed materials that were much more prone to cracking. It was as if they thought we should have thought of it earlier – and the more critical of our initial customers thought it was just a way of us making money.

But those customers are in the minority. Many initiators of new technology stay with what they have and play safe. We like to evolve, to improve and push the boundaries of creasing to the limit. And the vast majority of our customers love the fact that we always push to improve our technology – and that we address any disgruntlement by offering a buy back or part-exchange, where we take our old devices back for a generous fee if they upgrade to our latest and greatest.

That said, we still have devices in the market that are twelve years old. And the reason I took action against Rosback (aside from the fact that we pay good money to maintain our patents) was that I felt we had an obligation to take a stand for those customers who were still using the products and buying the associated consumables. Some of our U.S. customers still order the first phase devices and thankfully it remains superior to the device that Rosback came out with, which had key limitations imposed on it following the court case.

From that perspective it's damage limitation for us in that we still have a sizeable advantage in this area of the market, regardless of what any competitor is doing. (As an important side-note it's worth saying that people think it was a stroke of genius, a clever move by me to have created something that had a consumable element that could also be purchased from us, but it wasn't. It was really just an accident that it all evolved that way. But when I look at the sales figures, I'm glad it did. Consumables are a massive part of our business).

As a person who is so close to our technological progress, I have simply had to learn that whatever we come up with can potentially be bettered by any person who cares to evaluate it – those who hold our product in their hands and study how to design around the existing patents. That's just what happens in the innovation game and it isn't illegal. I have even managed to get around my *own* patents to improve them myself, in order to maintain our longevity in business. If I had stayed with my original design of 1998, I would be constantly worried that everyone would jump in when the patents expired. Instead, I reset my twenty-year patent clock in 2006 with a significantly improved version, and another twenty-year clock started in 2016 with the introduction of our latest and best solution yet – one that fully answers today's problems.

Any successful inventor or innovator of new technology must realise that if they create a ground breaking solution they will almost certainly create their own competition. They'll be continually feeding a greedy monster that starts to grow. How big the monster gets depends on a few things. But fundamentally it boils down to how much someone wants a slice of the market, and how much money the inventor has to try and stop them taking that slice. Sometimes the monster gobbles up the poor inventor, chews them up and spits them out – there is no mercy.

So, if you get into inventing and want to bring your creation to market yourself you need to think smart, not only in developing your solution but in developing your ideas to keep ahead of those that will try and capitalise on what you came up with. It's a race, and one that you can be proud to take part in. Remember, you have more knowledge than those in the race who don't bother to know what you know. They are the imitators. You can keep ahead, but you must first acknowledge how to use patents and protection to your best advantage.

And if things do go wrong...

Dealing With Adversity That Impostors Create... Like Losing A Major Court Case.

I remember having to wait five weeks for the press release from Rosback to come through, explaining their victory over us in our lawsuit. I spent much of this time mulling over in my mind what tone of response I was going to put out to the trade press because editors always like to get comments from both parties in such high profile cases.

As soon as the case was settled two or three press releases went out to U.S. print magazines; the details of the ruling were also posted on their news websites. In a strange way, I was proud to read the parts of the headlines that described my company as 'giants' or market leaders, but not so enamoured with the part that mentioned 'loss' or 'defeat'. What certainly felt good was that Rosback were making a big deal about the win – almost as if it was them who had kicked out at the shins of a Goliath. I couldn't help smiling at the irony of it all.

Firstly, we were, in relative terms at least, a small company – nothing like the giants we were being portrayed as in some circles. Secondly, at the beginning I used to think that it was us who were the David in the equation, pitting ourselves against the Goliaths of the industry and slowly carving out our own market share while ruffling the feathers of those who should or could have developed what we had. So while losing left a bad taste in my mouth, there was a sweet taste that came with it too: we were being acknowledged as a significant player in our market, and to look at it that way seemed like a good way of turning adversity on its head.

I often see creativity stifled by setbacks, companies often batten down the hatches and keep their heads low when other forms of adversity come along – like recession or economic downturn. I don't see it that way. In such times, I don't see problems; I see only opportunities. Much like my inventing is driven by a need to solve problems, I also love to think up ways of extricating myself from difficult situations. One thing I'm certain about is that there is no point in doing nothing. Paralysis isn't an option for me. As the narrative of this book will attest, it really isn't in my nature to play it safe and allow adversity to suffocate me. I love to be the person to come up with an obscure solution to a problem. I will never become separated from this; it is what makes me tick. I would rather quit altogether than keep my head down and wait for better times.

Having said all that, I know I have made mistakes, and in some cases they have been the reason why my company has lost hundreds of thousands of pounds, thus creating a degree of adversity at that time. But I also know that I have been the reason why we have made millions of pounds on the back of some good ideas and positive decisions. This isn't a boast, so please don't see it as that. I just created the freedom to do things the way I want with the backing of a good team. And I have sweated blood for the privilege. For that reason, no level of adversity can ever keep me down for long.

Consistent with that approach, I took full responsibility for this lost Rosback lawsuit and actually took it personally. It was my loss, my problem, and enough people had warned me about fighting this case in the first place. But as I've said, because I believe in protecting one's IP, I had no regrets. I'm proud that I stood up for my patents no matter the outcome. And the pleasant postscript is that, since we lost the case, it is reassuring to hear that Rosback's products have made little impact. I also heard that their U.K. Agent had approached the U.K. Heidelberg dealer and had been flatly rejected. My

Heidelberg contact, the guy responsible for assessing new developments told me that Rosback's demonstration was less than impressive and failed categorically. In my mind it felt like there is some justice after all!

Chapter 10

A Healthy Chip On My Shoulder

I LIKE to think that I've always carried that sort of 'healthy' chip on my shoulder, ever since I left school to work at Senator. As I alluded to previously, I've always felt a need to justify myself to the world, and in a strange way that inferiority complex has fuelled my work ethic. To that end, this chip has served me well over the years and I would encourage any inventor to acquire one.

Interestingly, when it comes to discussing what I do, I always feel a little awkward. It's such a strange thing because when I was young I felt exactly the same way about having to describe my work in the print factory. It *seemed* boring, and I didn't want to have to explain it in the pub. Now my life is anything but boring, and I *still* don't want to explain! Sometimes I just tell people that I have a business in the printing industry, and when pushed I just say that our company supplies solutions to the print trade. It seems easier to leave it like that.

When others ask what I do for a living, and I think to myself: *How can I make them understand?*

Or: *How do I even begin to describe my first flagship product, the Tri-Creaser?*

If I just say that I invented something, they inevitably ask what I invented. Out of sheer necessity I have a rehearsed line or two that basically tells them that I found a way to use an O-ring to crease paper so it doesn't crack when you fold it. I use the example of a greetings card. And then, as soon as I've said it, I think: *This sounds so sad!*

But it is what it is...

Occasionally people are quite intrigued and impressed, but more look at me as if I'd landed recently from another planet. They seem bewildered, and I often feel that they wish I'd said I created some amazing piece of software or an incredible household product like James Dyson did with his vacuum cleaner. Instead, in the same way as the simplicity of what I invented changed my industry, the simplicity of what I do every day often kills conversations. People seem underwhelmed, disappointed, and in some cases aggravated that it's not more complicated or exciting.

Even worse is the kind of look that many people in my profession have given me at times. It's that look that says they could easily kill me for coming up with something they think they could have done. Some have even told me that they came up with my idea before I had a patent. I think that most inventors of simple-sounding ideas get comments similar to this: folk being annoyed that they didn't do it before them. That's such a common feature of being a successful inventor: people think it's so easy... after you've made it. Not only did you create the product, but you also created the reaction where people dislike you for identifying something so simple. It's both hindsight and envy at work in those cases.

There are also people who love to hear the story of how I invented something that allowed me to travel and change my life. They ask so many questions and really hang on to my words. I like it when people appreciate something of what I've done, and to me it's the wider story that surrounds the inventions that's important, more than the products themselves – even though the solutions have changed the lives of many people.

All I really want to get across when people ask about my career is that I changed my path – and that that led to something different and more fulfilling. I'll always be pretty humble about the whole journey.

Unfortunately, I have seen so many inventors develop the bitter and arrogant type of chip – the kind that just makes them appear unprofessional and rude. That attitude puts investors off immediately. Inventors at print shows who have heard about my story sometimes approach me. These are usually everyday, normal people like me – who have done more than just talk about an idea. Some actually have a product on the go. I listened to one American guy who had developed an air filter system that fits onto the feeder of a folding machine to make the loading of sheets easier. I recognised it immediately as a luxury item in the context of our business – the kind of system that operators want, but there is no real advantage to their bosses (unless the sales guy is particularly good at persuasion and comes up with left-field angles like stopping repetitive strain claims from their workers or such like).

This particular inventor was good; he could talk the hind legs off a donkey. But he was really arrogant with it. He was boasting of various meetings he'd had with top U.S.A. manufacturers and he was loving telling me that his tough, straight talking, no-nonsense negotiations were going well. The trouble for him was that I knew some of the top guys at these companies. A few of them bought from us, and they told me a different story. They stated that it doesn't matter how great the product is, if they can't get on with the supplier (inventor) they won't bother at all.

My inventions have won three major awards at international business shows and I have met hundreds of inventors. Even now, some of the attitudes of these people amaze me. I have seen inventors with incredible products who couldn't be bothered to hone their pitch to present benefits and articulate the virtues of their creations. They tend to wear casual clothes and strut around the halls like peacocks, sending messages out to the rest of the competitors that they have the next technological gizmo that will change the world.

Then I see the same people go into depression because they were overlooked by the judges and by the tiny percentage of investors that passed them by. Somehow it seems that new inventors try to live up to that mad professor, quirky and scatty image – without having the inclination to learn any of the crucial business skills that must go hand in hand with a product.

Worse still, I have listened to inventors tell me, almost with pride, as though it is a badge of honour, that they have re-mortgaged their house or borrowed several thousands of pounds. These types of people really do think that an investor will come knocking on their door, and it rarely happens. I really think that inventors should stop thinking that they are ideas people that don't need to know about selling, they should get this type of precious mentality out of their minds.

Unfortunately invention show organisers and media alike feed into the mad professor scenario, it never fails to make me smile the amount of times I see bespectacled individuals plucked out by the organisers to be interviewed in front of cameras in their stripy suits and coloured boots with unmarketable ideas. It actually offends me.

In the early days, on the few occasions when I felt like talking to people about what I do, at a dinner party or in the local pub for example, someone always said to me, "Why wouldn't you just go on *Dragons' Den* and get funded and marketing help that way?"

I hear this all the time – usually from people who want a shortcut. The reality is that I applied twice to take part on *Dragons' Den*, and was asked to audition on both occasions. For those of you that know nothing at all about this cult TV show (U.K. version), entrepreneurs pitch for investment in the Den from the Dragons, five venture capitalists willing to invest their own money in exchange for equity.

My love for the show somehow compelled me to apply on-line, with the view to pitch one or two of my ideas just to see how I would fair against the formidable (or frightening) multi-millionaire business tycoons. I was flattered when a producer called me the first time I applied and asked if I could make my way over for the audition. And during that split second of silence that followed his question I could easily have accepted. After all, I have read every book written by the five Dragons at the time – and, if nothing else, it would have been my best chance to meet them all under one roof. However, the fact I *had* read all of their books meant that I knew that I wouldn't have been tolerated for more than ten seconds in that kind of forum. Read on and hopefully you will understand what I mean...

People often say to me things like "Graham, I'd love to see you pitch your Tri-Creaser on the *Dragons' Den*, just to see how you would get on."

Well that's just great for them, me being the focus of their amusement (well, for all of ten seconds anyway). Even my twenty-year old son has perfected the Scottish version of "I'm out," which was frequently muttered by Duncan Bannatyne – one of the previous Dragons on the show ("I'm Out" is the Dragons' catch phrase which essentially means, "Get lost, I won't be investing any money in you").

Of course, with such interest in how I may pitch to the Dragons mainly coming from my close family members and friends, all of whom just wanted me to grace their television screens and become instantly famous, maybe you can begin to see how I was tipped over the edge enough to fill out that application form in the first place (twice).

The trouble with the *Dragons' Den* is that you *can* actually become famous, but not necessarily for the right reasons. You can become *infamous* for not answering financial questions correctly, or for losing the ability to regurgitate well-rehearsed lines. This happens a lot, and Dragons and viewers alike are made to feel uneasy until the pitch gets back on track by the often-perspiring entrepreneur. Seemingly invincible young geniuses who, in my mind, would definitely go on to win the Nobel Peace Prize or become the next Richard Branson, are ridiculed and disgraced in front of the whole nation. Their ideas are picked to pieces and their credibility is shredded to bits. Yet sometimes (and only sometimes) I kind of see why: the Dragons don't take kindly to anyone that bluffs their way through a pitch, masks the truth or exaggerates the valuation of their unproven company, which may have absolutely no track record whatsoever.

If I'm really honest, the main reason why I find *Dragons' Den* so fascinating is because I know something of what the entrepreneur or inventor is going through. I know that their life has more than likely been consumed by the excitement that their idea has brought them, and I understand how people can actually believe they can become a millionaire overnight. I feel the frustration when a person standing before the Dragons is made to feel like a waste of space. My heart goes out to them.

When I started Tech-ni-Fold in 1999, I knew almost nothing about business. My first product was a bit like a scalding potato that had just come out of the oven and part of me wanted to hand it over to someone else as quickly as possible. Even my boss at the time advised me to sell my newly acquired patent to Heidelberg for a couple of thousand pounds or whatever I could get for it. He thought that it could pay for a nice family holiday. Thankfully I recognised its value as being a good bit more than that.

On the flip side, I once helped mentor a young man who invented an amazing product in the print industry, with good market potential. I advised in all the areas required to get his gadget on shelves. But the one critical piece of advice I gave him was ignored: the part concerning exclusivity. This guy had companies chasing him all over for his product, so he granted exclusivity to the biggest name in his field and is now tied into a restricted contract that hardly pays him a living.

The shame is that he handed over control because of flattery: them telling him how wonderful he and his product were and what great potential it had for both parties. Of course I have sympathy for and understanding of how this happens. Talented inventors often get sucked into a partnership that doesn't bring the true sales potential to life. Sometimes, like in this young man's case, the inventor asks the manufacturing partner to help pay the patent fees, thus giving them a hold over him. It only gets worse from there...

In some cases, granting exclusivity can be a great way to go, only if you get the returns that you feel are enough to give you the lifestyle you desire. But you'll need a lawyer to create the terms you want in order to achieve this, and both parties need to sign it. From there everything is easier, as the terms will stipulate sales targets and get-out clauses for if things don't go to plan.

All too often inventors are dazzled by the lights and feel they can trust the partner, without bothering with complicated or expensive paperwork like this. Then, six months into an unsigned exclusivity agreement when there are no sales, the inventor might want out. But then the manufacturer says, "Yeah but we've spent a fortune on advertising" and the inventor feels obligated to continue in a bad deal, afraid of the financial consequences. All of this can be avoided.

Earlier I spoke about how naturally lazy I am. But if I didn't discipline myself in key areas of law (where it is so easy to be lazy) then I would be dead in the water. I have certainly been drawn into some scrapes and been attracted to certain deals over the years, but I know from experience that nobody wants to make me rich. You need to engineer your own path, taking good advice in every aspect of business. Yes, I could have told myself that I have no qualifications of any kind and that inventing something is my one ticket, my only trick. But unfortunately it doesn't work out that way: running a successful business through invention demands many other skills, even if you have to learn them on the fly. So, if you know all this from the start, it will never be as bad as you think.

In a strange kind of way I did sit before Dragons of a sort, when I eventually faced Heidelberg after a successful testing of my invention the very next year (2000). A group of purchasing and product managers started to fill the room I had entered, and they made a point of getting negotiations under way with no little drama, thumping desks and all sorts. I was in a corner, but I didn't feel in any way cornered. Yes I was slightly pressurised, but I didn't succumb to it because I had the confidence of knowing that I had successfully sold two hundred of my creasing devices that had improved on anything theirs had done. I wasn't about to hand over my patent to anyone. I had something they wanted and I knew it, so it was a matter of working it all out from there.

This process took a couple of months, but it led to a purchasing contract that has lasted seventeen years thus far. Before I get myself into trouble with Heidelberg, I must say that they employed the right tactics to try and work with me. This is how business is, and we have enjoyed a fantastic relationship ever since, I promise!

But I'm not sure the Dragons would be quite so forgiving. There is nothing more annoying to the self made millionaires than someone who comes before them, no matter how great their idea may be, who wastes their time. Within a millisecond the Dragons would know that I wouldn't really need their investment, simply because my products are already a proven success. I even thought long and hard about ways in which I could pitch one of my experimental ideas, hoping I could use the Dragons' money to fund it and turn it into a separate business venture, separate from my more successful stuff. However, I know that from watching previous shows that people who try to do this are quickly exposed, and told that they too are insulting the intelligence of the panel.

That said, I am fortunate that *Dragons' Den* didn't exist in 1999 – 2001, as I am sure I would have applied to appear on the show, and gone through with it. I could have given away 40% of my business for the help that I thought I desperately needed at the time. Thankfully my story evolved the way it did, and now we have a second successful company, CreaseStream, and I wouldn't have had it any other way.

Shift Away From The Inventor Persona

So, having watched a few people get caught out in the Den and many more in real life business situations, I think it's vital that anyone going into invention should brush up on the business side of their venture as much as the innovation itself. At some point the 'inventor' tag must be shaken off if you're really going to make it, simply because potential investors or business partners won't take you seriously in that role alone. If you call yourself 'an inventor' when you walk into a business meeting, subconsciously you are taking on some of the familiar traits that the tag attracts. When you get quizzed on the finances, you could easily slip into that casual "I'm just the guy who invented it," mode. That just won't cut it.

To that end I would advise that if you are thinking seriously about selling your product yourself, or selling the concept to a manufacturer or investor you should first register as a company. You need to be more than what an inventor is perceived to be, and it is essential that you start to act like a serious business-person. Introducing yourself as purely an inventor, in my opinion, doesn't earn you the respect unless you use it as a tagline to you being a business-person.

I recently saw a news bulletin that showcased a very good invention in the DIY sector. The inventor sat hunched on a sofa in his casual jacket and jeans as he explained to the interviewer, in a monotone voice, how he'd ploughed over £60,000 into his product and how tough it had been to get his product tested and accepted in the five years he'd been trying. He then made a bizarre comment about him not doing it for the money, but mainly for the love of it! Although I truly admire this person, and I once met him at an invention fair and loved his invention, the interview did little to make him appear business savvy and astute – especially to potential manufacturer's who might consider giving him a call. I imagined B & Q executives or buyers seeing the interview and thinking: "We can probably get this product in at a snip because the guy who invented it is just happy to have even come up with the idea."

I also noticed that the interviewer's tone got quirkier as the interview went on, almost as slightly talking down to the inventor. Invention slots on programmes are always riddled with fun and humour, almost as though we are the court jesters waiting to be paraded for someone else's gratification. Sadly, we as inventors have often been more than happy to feed that monster because we seek attention and adulation for what we have done. But, if the person with the DIY invention had been introduced as a businessman, who acted and looked like a businessman that had just sealed another major contract with a DIY store, then I'm pretty sure that the guy interviewing him would have treated him with more respect.

I have exhibited at three invention shows over the years and won top awards each time by never looking like an inventor. I have dressed professionally and done my homework regarding how to present, speak to judges and interact with visitors. I am there as a businessman and not as an inventor, and I go there with winning top prize as my goal – so that, later, I can advertise in the print industry that my products are award winning. All of this points back to the business and generates more sales.

For the record, I have no doubt that, ten years or so ago, I could have probably done just the same as this inventor given the chance: I'd have gone on a show or a news slot, fed into the media circus and lived up to the image we all perceive of inventors. Now that I have been through my own journey and learnt so much more about business, I would love it if we could begin to change the perception. Or should I say, the *reality* we helped create regarding the inventors persona.

Nobody Can Make It Happen But You

Sadly, many creators of potentially good products don't seek publicity to generate interest in what they have produced. I would advise that if you have a patent pending that you find time to shout about it, doing everything you can to get it known. Demonstrate that *you* know the potential of your product and that *you* know its benefits and features. Become an expert and a font of knowledge, this will get you noticed and enhance other people's belief in not just your product but also you as a credible individual.

So, leave the Dragons to one side just now. Once you've reached the stage where you are ready to either present to would be investors, Dragons or otherwise, or show your new product at an inventor fair or trade show, the job is only half done. Here are a few tips I'd like to pass on that might make the process easier.

Make A Point Of Making A Good First Impression

I strongly advise against taking the slapdash approach to marketing materials and packaging that I initially took. I think we got away with it for a short time because the market was so desperate for the solution my device provided and some people warmed to my under-dog-with-a-great-idea story. Whether your brochure, website, and packaging come off as first-rate or second-rate, your product is likely to be judged accordingly. Put whatever resources you can toward putting forth a professional image from the outset. Then spruce it up later when you have the resources to do so.

Prove The Value Of Your Idea Before Reaching Out To Investors Or Manufacturers

I strongly urge any inventor or innovator to test market your idea and generate some sales *before* negotiating a deal with an investor, reseller, licensor, or distributor. Being able to provide real-life evidence of the benefits of your invention will help open doors and put you in a much stronger bargaining position. My naiveté in assuming that the big manufacturers would scoop up a first-of-its-kind device with no customer track record ended up working in my favour. Their rejection forced me to go out and find customers, who then put my device to work and proved its worth.

To Help Sell The Value Of Your Product, Show And Tell How It Beats The Competition

Always lead with the main benefit that sets your product apart from comparable products. Then point out the additional ways in which your solution provides added value – such as return on investment, ease of use, durability, warranty, technical support, good design etc.

Make Sure Your Product Is Market-Ready Before You Even Seek Publicity

Your product is ready to go to market when you have (1) sufficiently tested it to ensure it will perform as promised, (2) received your patent-pending notice, (3) named and priced your product, and (4) procured enough inventory and packaging to fill orders.

When I contacted *Printweek* after making my first sale, I still had not named my invention. Consequently, the article referred to my product simply as a "multiple-creasing device" – **and right there I missed my first branding opportunity**. Fortunately, by the time the story came out, the device had a name, the Tri-Creaser, and I printed the product name on the marketing leaflet and the user's guide.

Choose And Use Your Media Sources Wisely

It's always important to research which of the many media venues are popular with the people you want to buy, license, distribute, and/or invest in your product. Find out what types of stories your target media want and how to submit your press releases. Many media outlets post their editorial and submissions guidelines on their websites, but don't rely solely on those. Check out the publication or other media venue to get a feel for the nature and tone of their content.

Editors and journalists are typically too busy to

talk with you and depend solely on written press releases and article query letters, usually submitted via email. Follow their protocol and make sure your story idea is original, compelling, and relevant to their audience. Always address the editor or journalist by name and gear your pitch to their platform, indicating what their audience will gain from your story. Never send a generic e-blast or form letter, and don't hound the editor, producer, or journalist.

Give The Media Something To Talk About

Press releases, pitches, and submissions that merely announce a new product or trumpet the success of a business are a dime a dozen and unlikely to grab the attention of editors or readers. The media are always looking for human interest stories that showcase the *person* behind a success. I've found that editors and reporters love stories about the "little guy" who beat out the big guys in solving a problem or coming up with a unique product or business concept. Stories that highlight how a customer benefited from using your product are worth their weight in gold. In my experience, such customer testimonials are one of the most effective ways to build brand preference and generate leads.

Some publications favour stories about noteworthy achievements, such as landing a major customer or winning an industry competition. My products have won product design awards and my company has won a business innovation award, and I made sure to let all my media contacts know about each award. In the beginning, when the judges turned up at our garage to see my place of work, I wondered whether that would blow our chance, but they actually liked that about us and that we'd beaten multinational corporations. So did the reporters who included that information in their editorials, which their readers also enjoyed.

Be Prepared To Respond To Publicity Generated Leads

When someone is interested enough in your product to contact you, they expect you to be interested enough in them to respond promptly and appropriately. So it would benefit you to work out how you will handle incoming queries *before* the article, podcast, blog, television appearance, or other publicity even goes live.

I wasn't quite prepared for the reaction I got from my first editorial, which gave my home phone number "for additional information" (We had no website or email address at the time). Knowing I'd be at my day job when the article was published, I'd recorded a message on our answering device instructing the caller to leave a name and phone number and promising a prompt return call. The answering machine was full when I got home, and additional calls came in while I was there to answer them. That went on for five days. Who knows how many queries I missed because no one was there to answer the phone? And the message tape filled up before I could race home after work.

In my opinion and experience, relying on someone else to respond to queries is usually not the best approach. No one can match your knowledge and passion for your invention. There's an emotional attachment that only the inventor has so unless that person is the co-creator of your product, it simply can't mean the same to them. That said, you could still train someone to answer basic questions, take messages, schedule product demos and sales calls, and send brochures, spec sheets, videos, web links, or other information – or even free samples (if applicable). I strongly advise against relying on an answering device or service, unless you have no other option and then only on a temporary basis. Most prospective customers prefer talking with a real person anyway – and preferably without having to wait for a call back. The longer and more complicated it is to get the information they need to make a purchasing decision, the less likely they are to buy.

And if you *do* get a chance to exhibit somewhere...

Piggyback On Someone Else's Booth

Sharing a booth or being a guest exhibitor in another vendor's booth is a smart way to get some trade show exposure and experience, especially during the lean start-up years. Of course, you'll need to approach the other vendor (it's unlikely they'll come to you with the idea) and convince them there is a synergy between your business and theirs. So be prepared to point out how your gizmo complements their products and how you can add value to their trade show presence. The company owner or manager may want some form of exclusivity, limiting you to showcasing and selling your invention only at their booth. In most cases, you will need to pay a portion of the entrance and other exhibition fees, although you may be able to get on board for free if you help out. You will also be expected to provide your own marketing materials and cover the cost of your travel and any lodging expenses.

Inevitably, when you're successful in creating a marketable product, depending on the sector you're in, there may come a time where you may seek the involvement of other, perhaps more established partners. Well, I'm here to tell you that it's not always straightforward. Here's why...

In my industry, I witness all too often that the hierarchy in organisations that thrived twenty years ago are still calling the shots today. For some reason unknown to me, the owners of many of these companies just don't bring in young, new blood with modern ideas. This is such a tragedy. I'm not suggesting that all organisations operate like this, but it's no coincidence that a few of the companies that I have tried to work with over the years have some proud gatekeeper in place who revels in the role as company hero. Maybe they were responsible for the development of the product line in the past, and for that reason they're absolutely shut off to all new ideas. But the result is the same: the trail eventually goes cold.

Yes, they'll initially *speak* to you. They have to because their boss will have been cc'd on the email. Then what happens is very predictable. The boss tells the gatekeeper to check out a new idea, and then he tells his boss it is a no-go. Then the boss gets lost in all the technicalities and just supports his gatekeeper anyway. Conversation over. This is the sad side of what can happen, but as a new inventor this shouldn't put you off. You just need to find the good gatekeepers (there are usually quite a few) or go it alone, depending on what the situation and product calls for.

When I went to a U.S. based company, Baumfolder, a couple of years ago (the company that had dashed my dreams a decade and a half earlier) to show them the new feeding mechanism on our CreaseStream pro, the head of development and sales, or should I say the gate keeper, made a judgement call not to even consider it, just because it looked vaguely like something that his customers, in his opinion, would reject. That made no sense! It didn't seem to matter that it clearly solved the problem intended, and that it performed much better than the traditional vacuum methods.

What was worse was that this gatekeeper had been specifically asked to look at alternative methods of digital finishing because the machine they were promoting was too expensive and didn't sell. Our feeder did as intended, transporting the sheets without marking them to the tooling shaft where the sheets were creased accurately with no cracking, better and faster than their solution and for half the price. What wasn't there to love? His staff raved about it; his boss was excited to do business, but the gatekeeper did all he could to discourage it.

...And, sixteen years previously he also rejected my original Tri-Creaser, telling me that his company already had something better. Despite that, for the last twelve years he has been purchasing the Tri-Creaser and many of our other products, directly from Technifold U.S.A., at more than double what he would have paid had he secured the exclusive deal with us that he was offered. I know that his colleagues think he is crazy – I can see it in their faces. They know that they missed a great opportunity, but because their gatekeeper had developed machines 25 years ago, (and it doesn't matter that they don't sell so well any more) he is the main man and still calls the shots. These situations occur all too often.

Regardless, I spent three days locked in meetings with him, and while I was over there, not only did we prove that our feeding system didn't mark digital materials (this guy kept throwing stock after stock at me to try and trip us up) but we also proved that our creasing was superior to a traditional method they sold. He and his colleague tried everything they could to make their product appear to perform better. They produced sheets and sheets of material that they thought made their case.

It's not usually in my nature to score points, but on this occasion their attitude was such that I couldn't resist doing a couple of comparisons that led to one of the guys looking really stupid. Anyone could see that our creasing was superior, and with that they backed off and apologised for their unpleasant approach. Really, looking back, I was treated very badly.

These guys had merely been flexing their muscles however; that's not uncommon. And I had felt that it was becoming unnecessarily personal. In addition, it seemed that there was a background explanation to this attitude of theirs, aside from me.

Prior to their attempted points-scoring performance, when the Vice President of the company showed me around the site, I noticed just a handful of workers scattered around a massive factory. It was quite a strange sight. I knew what the signs of company demise looked like; I'd seen them first hand myself in the past. The truth of the matter was, this company, on whom I'd done a lot of homework, was obviously struggling. It appeared that they had elected to stay safe, eschewing any kind of evolution, which, by extension was exemplified by their unwillingness to work with me.

Despite getting on great with the Vice President, who wanted to work with me, I lost my enthusiasm because of the gatekeeper's attitude, and I told her that he was a concern.

Fortunately I was in a position where I didn't *have* to do business with this company, but both the Vice President and I could see the obvious benefits to both parties. I liked her outlook, she was so positive in her thinking that her company could reinvent themselves in the industry. What's more, I truly believed we could have helped them do it. But the gatekeeper stood in the way – the same one who, sixteen years earlier, had told me straight out that my Tri-Creaser wouldn't succeed. He did so after building me up for a while, toying with me, and then crushing my young dreams. But they were only crushed temporarily. History shows that we sold tens of thousands of devices into the U.S.A..

So what's the message in all of this if you're new to inventing?

Well, when I went back to Baumfolder with Creas-eStream, I didn't need to work with this company. The only reason I made contact again at all was that I'd read that the Vice President was actively seeking collaborations. As I said, when we connected, I liked her, and she explained that she was a great admirer of our technology. But here's the important bit.

As much as Baumfolder were one of the biggest folding machine manufacturers in the U.S, by that time a lot of water had flowed under my business bridge since I first encountered them. No longer was I the Graham Harris of old, a lone innovator trying to clinch a dream deal in the land of opportunity. This time it was a meeting that was held openly with both parties free to express their concerns and to evaluate the potential of

243

a two-way collaboration. Really I was evaluating them as much as they were casing me. And now I had a voice as strong as theirs. I saw myself as equal to them now, and I had every right to feel that way. But regardless, the gatekeeper killed any possibility of a successful alliance. What a shame that is for both parties.

Chapter 11

Letting go of the reins a little and the way forward

"If you really want to grow as an entre-preneur, you've got to learn to delegate"
— Richard Branson.

ONE OF THE toughest parts of growing a successful business is when the founder who got it started has to hand over some of his or her responsibilities to someone else. Having said that, it is a crucial part of the process and in my opinion can be the difference between your company just keeping afloat or racing ahead of the competition. Trying to do it all yourself can break you, whilst choosing your staff wisely will make you. It is as simple as that.

For the record, it was doubly difficult for me because I had to allow someone else to take on the one thing I loved more than anything – the day to day hands on development of new products, whilst I focused on sales and marketing. That someone, Paul, was someone who left a huge impression on me when our paths first crossed.

Paul was the technical specialist at Senator and as part of that he used to configure and link all sorts of machinery together to process complex jobs that came to the company. He also helped train some of the younger guys – his innovative approach was something special and he stood out, and unlike me he was a time served apprentice, with the papers to show for it.

Unlike me, inventing from scratch wasn't exactly what Paul did. Instead he worked out how to get work processed using what was available at Senator and like all of us he improvised to get the job done. When Paul came to Tech-ni-Fold, he brought along his work ethic and unique mind-set. He learned fast and could install the few products I had developed. Above all, Paul and I are on the same wavelength when we create solutions, and I would like to think he has a similar high level of respect for me, as I have of him. Paul can assess any given machine and work out how to apply our technology, in whatever format it turns out to be. Sometimes Paul will combine ideas and stretch boundaries.

When it comes to improving our technology, it is usually driven by customer feedback, because we keep our ears to the ground and address any issues – especially if we keep getting the same message coming through again and again. Obviously, we sometimes don't know straight away how to solve a problem; we just know what the problem is. In our industry, print applications change constantly as does paper/stock manufacturing, and sometimes combining the two together can change the rules of creasing. Brittle recycled paper and varnished print create problems and that's good news for us, what we developed sixteen years ago to combat cracking issues just wouldn't hold up when applied to digitally printed materials today, we are always evolving, improving and moving forward.

Often I will come up with a project to address a problem that occurred on more than one occasion. In most cases I will first ask Paul to try some things and then get involved myself if they don't work. Sometimes, like with CreaseStream, it takes us 2-3 years to configure how to do it, and it usually ends up being really simple, just like all the great ideas. I think that Paul and I complement each other and always get the problem solved, one way or another. Paul is more grounded and cautious. I am the opposite. When I'm inventing, I don't think about logic or price or circumstances. I want the result to come fast once I've committed to seeking it out. Paul is the opposite. He keeps things calm and settled and weighs up all the options, He knows that everything takes at least twice as long to develop than you think – that's just how things turn out.

With CreaseStream in particular, I had done a lot of the forethought and thinking in advance. But it still needed hours and hours of Paul's hard slog to convert my theories into practical realities. This is why Paul is so special: he pays attention to every small detail – details that I often overlook when I'm in full flight.

At first my idea had been to deploy Paul into the development side of my company to replicate what I had done – to make bigger and smaller versions of Tri-Creasers to fit different types of machines, and the same applied to my micro-perforating and cutting tools. He then progressed to adapting variations of the devices on special applications. And he then took on the responsibility for sales in the U.K.

As it turned out, the customers were driving Paul's innovation just like they had done with me previously. Meanwhile I had time to find better suppliers and work on new concepts that often led to new patents and meanwhile Paul worked hard to make them work. Basically we pooled our resources and the formula worked very well, it still does. Under my direction Paul has developed over 600 adaptations of solutions within the confines of various patents we took out. He has been the go-to guy for our customers for a long time, while I've been content to step back and let him be that. He has been, in many ways, the front man for Tech-ni-Fold in the sense that so many people have relied on him to solve problems, including several of our distributors.

Paul never lets anyone down, he works tirelessly and has recently opened up an exciting opportunity in a different field that is doing really well. He has been a significant contributor to helping Tech-ni-Fold reach the high level of success that we have. But all good things come to an end, and Paul is due to retire in December 2017. He'll leave a massive gap that Sue and I have already given thought to how we'll fill.

My son Jack is in the business now and has taken over the reins of the CreaseStream arm of the business to the extent that I have real confidence in his ability to take it forward in the way I would have. He doesn't know everything yet, but he's young and is learning. It'll come in time. I should say that I didn't in any way pressurise him to join the business. I left it entirely up to him. And the same applies to Sophie. They've both been to University, seen a bit of life and have become two incredibly well rounded people that I'm incredibly proud of. If they decide that they want to make this business their lifelong career, I'll support them in that as much as I have in everything else. But the choice is theirs.

It is profoundly important to emphasise at this point in my book that no matter how much passion and determination I have exercised in product development and innovation, I would never have realised my true potential, and our company would never have reached these dizzy heights without the support of an entity that possesses a richness of key business skills I lack, and believe me I lack quite a few. My incredible wife Sue is not only that entity, but she also transcends a positive force that threads its way all through our whole team and extends far beyond. She is extremely business savvy – more so than I am – and holds us all together. Having someone so close through the ups and downs of business with such a positive attitude is incredible – it takes a lot of pressure away from me.

Furthermore, Sue's accounting skills and understanding of the financial side of the company have been and still remain paramount to our success, she organises and runs the office and maintains high levels of business administration, yet she shuns the limelight, instead selflessly building a platform for me to continue doing what I love to do. Sue backed me and my dreams from the start and worked those long hours into the night to make sure our business had everything in place: invoices going out to customers and making sure our suppliers got paid on time. I am hugely indebted to her – and it wasn't always easy with two young children to look after. Sure, I like to think I come up with some big product ideas, but equally Sue has executed many of her own, her decision for Tech-ni-Fold to go into mail order and take our customers money up front before sending them the product was a masterstroke, despite my initial objections.

In business we are worlds apart. Sue is meticulous and organised and I am very often the opposite. However we do have our fingers on the pulse in our own areas. We sometimes hold mini business meetings whilst walking our dog, or driving home, and can often disagree with each other. But whatever big decision we make together, always seems to be the right one.

Sue is the ever-present rock without which none of what has gone before could possibly exist. Without her I might not have been writing this! We are extremely proud of what we have achieved with our company but that's only part of what life is about. There is a bigger purpose that drives us, born out of our faith. We stand together in doing what we can, through our charity organisation, to help other less fortunate people, in our church and community. This is an area Sue and I will start to dedicate more time during this period in our lives, supporting more projects that can change lives.

So what now?

You've read my story, you've seen how I, Graham Harris, the most normal of normal people transformed my life.

Do you want to do the same, and I mean *really* want to?

If you do, be afraid of remaining as you are, content, safe. Picture a version of you, thirty years down the line and ask yourself if you like what you see. If you don't, keep being afraid. Be scared of being put on the shelf – or of being put in a box by work colleagues or friends who think they've got *your* life story all figured out.

Don't use laziness as an excuse for anything. Instead, use every ounce of strength you have to pull yourself out of that, resigned, comfortable chair for life. Once you've done that, you just need to engage the attitude that will help identify that one incredible thing that will change your life forever. Trust me, when you do, your renewed vigour for life will drag your idle soul through all the hoops you'll need to jump through.

What's also certain is that the decision to make a change now that will alter how your life turns out, won't be as difficult as you think. It's actually very simple: all you must do is commit to following your dreams. But you've got to *genuinely* want it, not just have a vague, "Let's see what happens, I suppose…" type of mentality. That's just setting up for failure.

If I told you that the correct state of mind is just as

crucial as finding a problem to solve out in the world, I wouldn't be exaggerating. So start putting yourself in that headspace now, even in your current situation. Don't give up your job; don't give less to your job; respect those that pay your wages. But at the same time be smart and pour your spare time into new thinking. Love every moment and start acting like you are on a mission on which you can't fail. Control your emotions, be patient and believe you can do it.

Once you find that enlightened state I'm referring to, I'm certain you will see alternative and better ways to improve or create things. You will surprise yourself. If you are at home for whatever reason, look around, look outside for something to fix that no one has addressed, improve something that niggles at you, that people might want. Open your mind, relax and have fun. Remember, once I decided to solve a problem, it took me less than a month to do it and it changed my life forever. You can do exactly the same.

As a child you were curious and asked so many questions, admit it – we all love to hear parents being bombarded with questions they can't answer by someone less than their waist height. But through our school years the asking by the child is replaced by being told to shut up and listen, by teachers telling us how it is. This is called conformity, and it's also how creativity is silently killed. But now's the time to reverse that trend. Reinvent that child-like behaviour you once had, ask those questions that no other adult dare ask, risk sounding stupid, because stupid is only temporary. Who says that something you look at in your world cannot be deconstructed and made to work better, faster or more efficiently? Says who?

One night recently I was emphatically reminded

how life's twists and turns can affect the way our life can turn out when you take the plunge – how even a negative situation that was tough to take at the time turned out for the better, and how I am so pleased that it happened this way. Let me explain...

I bumped into the guy (at our local pub) who beat me to a managerial job at a large printing company, three months before I developed my Tri-Creaser. Had I got that job I am almost certain my focus would have turned to that new challenge, and with that the chances of my creating my own path might have disappeared. I was disappointed for a while, not to have succeeded in getting the job, of course I was. But at the same time, I was already of the mind that I could instigate some alternative opportunity for myself some day. I guess that for me, I didn't have his overall print knowledge and that fact had haunted me in that it was like I wasn't worthy of landing a job above my station. I remember thinking to myself that maybe someone will find me out and realise that I wasn't the perfectly tutored apprentice that most people who land such positions are.

That night, we caught sight of each other whilst passing in the pub and we both adopted that "Don't I know you?" look before exchanging a few pleasantries. As it turned out, this gentleman had, a few years ago, bagged a nice job at the National Printing Skills Centre – a place where he devised training methods for print students. This made me smile because, earlier in my career, I had given *my* free time to help set up that department at its inception. I even wrote a programme about print finishing and had rather hoped that I would be given the full time role to head this programme up when it launched. But that call never came.

At the pub at that moment, I saw the grey haired

version of how I could have turned out had I achieved the qualifications and acquired those papers he held – or if somehow I had been chosen in at least one of those jobs instead of him. He was talking about how cushy his job was and how he was looking forward to scaling down his career. He said there was no challenge left, and that he no longer had any passion for the job he held. His face was that of someone who was just winding down the clock on his working life.

As I looked at him, I was shocked – for all the right reasons. This guy went the conventional route and achieved the career I once thought I wanted. How close I came, but I suddenly realised that not being trained or schooled in a conventional way had led me into a much more exciting adventure, away from conformity and away from that feeling of wanting to wish the last years of a career away. I had once envied this guy, even if only until my Eureka moment came about. Right then I felt so grateful that he'd beat me to those jobs because by doing so helped me change the course of my own life forever.

Don't get me wrong, this guy was clever, loved his family, was very happy and had clearly achieved a lot of things in his career. I'm sure he worked hard and had pushed himself to do better, and that, to me, is always to be respected. But I wouldn't swap places for anything. I wouldn't swap places with many people.

On that subject, interestingly, I've never really considered myself to be the kind of guy who looked up to many people or had any particular mentors. Recently though, for one reason or another, I've started realising that maybe I do after all.

I had a dream while I was in Dubai on a short break. Inexplicably, a person who meant a lot to me during my years at Senator Print Finishers popped up in it. His name was Trevor Reynolds. Looking back, Trevor was one of the people that I really respected in my professional career. I think many of the people that knew him would say the same thing. He really was the most naturally gifted print finisher I had ever met. He had that magic touch that could somehow cure any problem that any of the best finishing specialists in our company ever encountered.

The most exasperating thing about Trev was that he didn't show any kind of passion for his job. For him it was just a means to an end, but instead he seemed to genuinely love horse racing and used to send the young trainees over to the bookies to place his bets. What an incredible character. Yet despite his seeming lack of love for the trade, we all had an amazing respect for him. For me he was in the Steve Hackney class of 'Guruism' (maybe I just invented a word): a specialist who accomplished the most difficult tasks with the least amount of effort. Trevor had the natural skill sets associated with the folding machine I so desired. I spent considerable time trying to avoid having him stroll over to my machine to tweak something that made finished work so much better in an instant. We all had to succumb to this, and he never failed to fix any problem. He was a magician.

At Senator, I'd decided from an early stage that if I wasn't going to be as good as Trevor from a skill perspective, I'd do everything I could to grab his attention and earn his respect, which wasn't easy. In fact, other than when he ambled over to nonchalantly fix a problem without breaking stride, it was hard to get his attention at all. Trev was too busy pacing up and down the factory floor, checking his pockets for betting slips as he went, while lighting a cigarette with his free hand (amazingly, in those days, smoking was allowed in print factories). With his shirt often hanging out, he was the closest approximation to Columbo, the famous TV detective of that era, that I'd ever known, but he sadly passed away a few years after I left.

In this dream Trev was banking on me to set up a complex finishing job and I badly wanted to accomplish it to meet his approval. I was really struggling, but at the same time I didn't want him to have to intervene. Although it was a dream, it felt like even he knew that I wanted to do this myself and he was patient with me – perhaps allowing me more time than he might usually have to get there. My dream moved on and I saw my machine running and that the resulting work was of average quality. But I tweaked it and made it right, while Trev gave me his nod of approval and ambled on. The dream told me one important thing: Trevor is a mentor after all. He is still one of my main motivational drivers and I'd like to think he would be proud of me.

Furthermore, when my mood is low for a day or so because of a life situation or a troubling business issue, I've found that I tend to have other dreams that involve people who I have looked up to and respect the most. Sometimes I dream about my mum and dad and it comforts me in difficult moments, because they had gifts and traits I so admired. But the biggest dream of all is the one that never ends. It's the one where I, Graham Harris, the young man full of self-doubt and insecurity, who made the decision to go against the grain and live a different life from the guys that sat beside me, eyes fixed on the clock, complaining, on the pallets at the back of the print factory.

Now, at the age of 54, with everything you've read

in this book behind me, the dream goes on while I live in a community of similarly aged people who dream about retirement and doing things they can't do now. I don't yet feel that way. I love getting up in the morning to continue this amazing adventure. For me, the chase goes on...

Acknowledgements

I thank God for every page written in this book. I often thought Sue and I could cope with everything that came our way, but when things got really tough it was you that got us through. Of course, Sue is my rock, not only as my best friend and beautiful wife, but also as a wonderful and talented business partner who has been and still is a huge driving force behind our business success on so many levels - I love you Sue, and know that this journey would not have been even remotely possible without you remaining firmly by my side every step of the way.

We both know that without our talented team, who have contributed enormously – most of whom took a risk to change career paths completely – that the journey wouldn't have been so much fun, or half as successful - thank you Paul Barrett, Wendy Austen, Lee White, Trevor Warren, Steve Humphreys, Tristan Owen and our son Jack. In fact I am so excited that Jack, who with our daughter, Sophie will have a huge impact on our business moving forward. Thank you both for inspiring me, I love you both dearly – and I'll never forget how you both passed me the ruler and paper as young children and helped me sketch up my first product idea. Sue and I would like to thank all of our close family who have inspired us through our journey.

A massive thank you to Gina and Andre Palko – who lit up North America with their passion to sell our products. You are two truly gifted people who took a chance coming on board. You both have inspired Sue and I ever since. You remain special friends who never fail to demonstrate positivity and a high degree of determination in everything you do. Thank you Uwe Reimold for being an amazing business partner and friend - one of the very best we have had the privilege of working with.

A huge thank you to Mark Eglinton who helped me piece together this book, you have been inspirational and so encouraging, every step of the way, and taught me so much about writing.

Thank you to my publisher, Rudling House, for taking my book on. Karen Butler has been amazing and has worked so hard to make this happen. Having such an exciting and forward thinking publisher with a solid reputation, who already supports some great authors, is truly inspirational.

And last, but by no means least, Rev Mark Clay, thank you for your encouragement and belief in me, from the start, and for reminding me that faith can move mountains!

- Graham